Biblical Easter and Spring Performances

Stories, Choral Readings, Poems, Plays, Musicals and Songs

Compiled by Rebecca Daniels
illustrated by Janet Skiles

Cover by Janet Skiles
Shining Star Publications, Copyright © 1989
A Division of Good Apple, Inc.
ISBN No. 0-86653-478-4
Standardized Subject Code TA ac

Printing No. 9876
Shining Star Publications
A Division of Good Apple, Inc.
Box 299
Carthage, IL 62321-0299

TO THE TEACHER/PARENT

Biblical Easter and Spring Performances is a book overflowing with joyful stories, choral readings, poems, plays, musicals, and songs written especially for young performers. You may be planning an informal recitation for a small family gathering in your living room or a huge musical play with song presentations to be delivered to hundreds of people, on stage, with costumes and scenery; or your Easter performance plans may fall somewhere in between. But no matter which selections you choose to perform, the children are sure to dazzle the audience and have them standing in ovation when they present any of the performances found on the following pages.

Begin your plans by carefully reading all the selections herein. Make careful note of the selections you like best. Read some (or all) of them to your children. Let them help you decide which they would like to present this Easter. The performance is sure to be a huge success if the children have their hearts and hands in the selection of materials to be presented.

Reproduce the playscripts, choral readings, poems, songs, etc., as needed for your group of children. Make sure there are plenty of rehearsals so that everything will go smoothly on stage! Costume suggestions and backdrop patterns that can be enlarged for scenery are included in the last chapter of the book to add that special touch to your Easter presentation. This Easter help children discover the true meaning of the Easter story as they hear and perform the Bible-based selections herein.

TABLE OF CONTENTS

EASTER STORIES

Shining Star Publications, Copyright © 1989, A division of Good Apple, Inc.   SS1869

THE ART OF STORY-TELLING

The art of storytelling has been cultivated in all ages among people who have left any records. It is an outcome of instinct that seems to be planted universally in the human mind.

Stories were told by mothers of the wildest tribes as well as those of the more advanced races. Little ones were hushed to sleep by stories. Weary hunters often sat around a fire amusing themselves with curious tales of the hunt.

Children have great imaginations. They can easily imagine that clouds are boats, dogs or mountains according to their shapes or sizes. One child asked the teacher if clouds were angels' clothes. So with such imagination in the minds of an audience, the storyteller is right at home.

In earlier years there was usually one person in every community who excelled in the art of storytelling, someone whose imagination and memory was exceptionally good. This person was in great demand and never lacked for listeners.

Today we have so many wonderful books and magazines for children. Anyone can be a good storyteller with a little practice. One does not need to do a story without a book, but should be able to carry on with it by looking at the listeners while reading. The voice should sound as though the teller is speaking, rather than reading.

The following suggestions may help the beginning storyteller to a successful achievement:
1. Be thoroughly familiar with the selection to be interpreted.
2. Learn to create moods, impressions.
3. Read dramatically but naturally.
4. Use gestures, pauses, changes in rate of reading.
5. Develop the ability to keep children as good listeners. If they become restless after a short period of time, present a dramatic pause, using facial expression, as if to say "Wonder what comes next?"

Children in small groups make a better audience, but a good storyteller can hold the attention of a large group. It takes practice, proper projection of voice, perfect enunciation and timing. If this can be accomplished, no microphone will be needed. Teach children to listen by the storytelling method. It really works!

After children have enjoyed a story, let them dramatize it in their own fashion: pantomime while the story is being read, rewrite the story as a play. (Even children in first grade can do this in the simplest form.)

Children also enjoy taking an idea from a story and developing their own story. The more writing children do the better developed their imagination will become. The students of today need all the creative writing they can get from first grade on through school.

　　　　SS1869

PALM SUNDAY

by Marion Schoeberlein

Phillipa was very excited about festival day in Jerusalem.

"Father, may I go along this year?" she asked.

"I think you are old enough to enjoy the festival now," her father answered.

"Will there be dancing and feasting?"

"Of course there will be dancing and feasting. That is what festivals are!" her mother laughed.

Phillipa knew her parents would take figs and olives and wine to the festival. They always did.

I'm glad my father is well-to-do, she thought. Having so many olive groves has made him rich.

I will have a new mantle for the festival, a silk one embroidered with flowers. It will be so much fun to dance at the festival, and maybe Father will even let me drink some wine.

Dorcas, Phillipa's best friend, was dreaming about the festival, too. "They say it will be the biggest one Jerusalem has ever had," she told Phillipa, "and they say a man by the name of Jesus is coming. That will make the crowds even bigger, because some will come just to see Him."

"Who is Jesus?" Phillipa asked.

"Some say He is a prophet. Some say He is

SS1869

the Son of God," she smiled, "and He can perform miracles."

"Really? My father would not believe in a man who says He can do miracles. He says there is only one God and that is Jehovah."

"I know, but many still believe in this man. He is very popular," Dorcas said.

"Well, I am going for the feasting and the dancing," Phillipa clapped her hands, "and not for this Jesus!"

Phillipa and her parents were on the way to the festival. She felt very beautiful in her purple mantle.

"You look almost a woman today," her father said.

"Soon now she will find a husband," her mother teased.

"Look, Father, there is a man riding ahead of us on a donkey," she laughed. "What a way to come to the festival! He must be very poor!"

Following after him were a few meek-looking men who might have been fishermen or tentmakers. They looked dusty and tired.

"I think that is the man they call Jesus and those are His disciples," her father explained.

"Is that Jesus?" Phillipa asked. "I want to get up closer and see Him, Father. Dorcas has told me all about Him. He is supposed to do miracles."

"Nonsense. That is propaganda, Phillipa. But if you really want to see Him I suppose we can leave our carriage here and walk the rest of the way to Jerusalem."

Phillipa hugged her father. "Yes, Father, I am very curious to see Him," she said.

This was going to be more interesting than the festival. Ahead of them a crowd was gathering. They had palm branches in their hands.

Phillipa hurried ahead of her parents.

Now the crowd was chanting something.

They spread their palm branches in the man's way. As she came closer, Phillipa heard the words they were chanting:

"Hosanna! Blessed is the King of Israel that cometh in the name of the Lord!"

Jesus' face shone. There was light in it and poetry and kindness. Phillipa had never seen a man like that before.

Maybe He can do miracles! she thought.

The donkey stopped, but Jesus did not descend. The men with Him tried to push the crowds away.

Phillipa brushed against Jesus' white robe. I am happy to be so close, she thought. Maybe He will say something to me. But He didn't. The man, Jesus, looked as if He was from another world, as if He had some great and wonderful plan on His mind.

I'll give Him a palm branch, too, she thought, and found one in the path.

She put it in Jesus' hand. He smiled. Phillipa would never forget that smile.

When her parents found her, they were angry.

"Why did you run ahead of us?" they asked. The crowd was pressing. It could have been dangerous."

"I'm sorry, but I just had to see Him," Phillipa explained. "I had to put a palm branch in His hand."

"We must be on our way to the festival now," her father urged. "I thought that was the most important thing to you today."

"It was, Father, until I saw Him. I have never seen a face like that." She picked up one of the palm branches that was strewn in the road.

"I want to take it home with me," she said. "I think I will remember Him much longer than the festival."

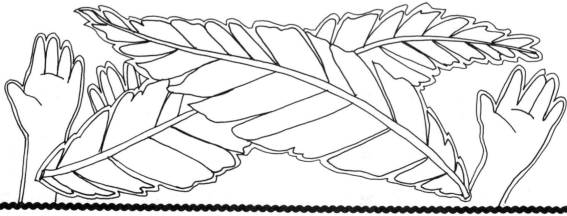

SS1869

AT THE SECOND CROW OF THE ROOSTER

by K. H. Munn

Rebecca was tired. She had worked all night at the home of the High Priest, cleaning off tables, washing dishes and generally preparing for the activities of the next day.

But this was her job, and it helped her mother pay the bills following the death of her father. She busied herself with the chores, trying to keep awake and alert—and out of trouble.

The worst part of this, she thought yet again, is that it's so hard to sleep in the daytime, with the children playing and the sun streaming in the window. But worst of all was Rusty, their old rooster, who was always crowing. Her mother had promised to have him for dinner soon, and she could hardly wait for the crowing to stop—permanently. The crowing started with the first rays of sun in the morning and he didn't quit until every chicken in the flock was safely on the roost in the evening.

She looked out of a nearby window then, wondering how close it was to time for the sun to come up that day. She could just see the buildings across the way, becoming visible in the early morning light. As she watched, a group of people came down the lane, and one man, lightly bearded and of medium height—just an ordinary looking man—was being pushed along by a soldier. The man looked sad, she thought, and she wondered what he had done. Not far from him was another man, also with a sad face, shuffling along through the dust and watching what was happening. And there was a third man, a young fellow, following close behind the man under

 SS1869

arrest, speaking to him in a sympathetic way. As they passed the open window, a guard grabbed at the young fellow, as if to arrest him too, but he ran back the way he had come. Huh, she thought, I wonder what's happening?

After the young man ran off, the soldier that had tried to grab him walked over to the second sad-looking man. She could hear him through the open window as he said, "What's your name? And why are you here with this Nazarene?"

The man looked directly at the soldier. "My name's Peter, and I'm just walking along the lane. Is that against the law?"

The soldier looked at him hard, but left again to guard the prisoner.

Just then the son of the High Priest entered the room. "That's the Nazarene they just arrested," he said, pointing out of the window. "I think his name is Jesus. He claims to be the Son of God."

Jacob, for that was his name, then looked up at the sun above the buildings across the way and said, "You had better get home and rest up Rebecca. Dad will be needing you again tonight."

He's nice, she thought. And smiling quietly, she let herself out of the front door, waving gracefully at Isaac as she left.

She went off down the lane, walking the short distance to the small path leading home. Just beyond the path was a fence surrounding the courtyard of the building where the courts of law met. She heard voices coming from inside the fence. Being a curious girl, she walked over to the gate, which was open, and looked in. There, at the opposite end of the courtyard, near the building, stood the man called Jesus, surrounded by judges dressed in judicial gowns, shouting in angry voices. Jesus' face was not frightened, but she thought he looked sad. And near her, in a group of bystanders, was the man that had called himself Peter. He had a different look about him, similar to the Nazarene, and this made her wonder. So she said to him, "You're dressed like the prisoner,

Jesus, and you were with him."

But Peter responded, "I don't know what you mean," and just as he said it Rebecca heard old Rusty crow.

This puzzled Rebecca, she looked at one of her neighbors standing nearby. "He was with him," she said.

Her neighbor peered closely at Peter. In a mean and angry way he said, "Becky saw you, you *were* with him!"

"Why would I be with him? I don't even know the man," said Peter, but he felt really sad inside after he had said it.

Hearing all the loud talk, another man, standing by a fire nearby warming his hands, for it was still early morning, looked around and he, too, peered closely at Peter. "Yes, you were with him alright. I saw you. I'm sure of it."

For the third time that morning Peter denied Jesus; he cursed and said, "I swear, I never met the man." And old Rusty crowed for the second time of the day. Peter's face crumpled when he heard the rooster's crow. Rebecca saw Jesus look towards Peter, a look of deep sorrow on His face. Peter saw too, and covered his face with his hands. Tears flowed out between his fingers and he cried out, "Oh Jesus, my Lord and Savior, forgive me. You were right, I *did* deny you." He found his way through the gate and went stumbling down the lane, back the way he had come.

Rebecca felt terrible for the man. Tears came to her eyes as she watched him make his way home, crying out in anguish as he went. And the tears ran down her cheeks as well—great salty drops falling onto the dry, dusty ground of Jerusalem.

SS1869

PASSOVER FOR JOSHUA

by Lenore Kurz

It was Joshua's favorite time of year. People came from all over to Jerusalem to celebrate Passover. For the next week they would celebrate with carefree abandon in spite of the presence of Roman soldiers. Every day his father would take him to the temple. After they prayed, Joshua's father would be occupied with the other Pharisees and Joshua was free to explore.

First he would go to the money changers and watch them. It was fascinating to watch how quickly their hands moved and to listen to them talk so fast. They would soon get annoyed with him watching and chase him away. This day they were not in their usual spot, but instead, far outside the temple. Someone had chased them. Someone named Jesus of Nazareth, whoever he was.

He came to the place where Old Ben sat. Before leaving home that morning, he tucked a matzoh and some figs into his pouch for Old Ben. He was sure nobody else was concerned if Old Ben had anything for Passover. At the beginning of the week, Joshua asked his mother if he could bring the old, blind beggar home for the Seder. But, his mother had told him that they had many important guests invited and Old Ben just would not fit in. But today Old Ben was nowhere to be found. Joshua began to search for him; he asked everyone where Old Ben was. It was amazing how many people had never taken notice of an old, blind beggar. Others simply said, "Good riddance."

SS1869

A shepherd boy from nearby Bethlehem, no bigger than himself, led four lambs to sell for temple sacrifices. They were perfect, without a blemish, the boy proudly pointed out to Joshua, and should bring a good price. But no, he had not seen an old, blind beggar. Joshua patted one of the lambs and quickly moved on. Their innocent faces made him feel sad.

Suddenly he saw Old Ben in the marketplace, but he was not sitting down with his cup. His eyes were open and he was looking around with wonder as he went from merchant to merchant, examining all the wonderful things they had to sell—seeing them for the very first time in his life.

Joshua had to rub his own eyes to be sure he was awake and really seeing correctly. He ran up to the old man, who did not know what he looked like. Ben recognized Joshua's voice immediately, and the two friends embraced warmly. Joshua listened eagerly as Old Ben shared the good news of Jesus and all he had done. "Why don't you know about Jesus?" asked Ben. "Weren't you here the other day when he rode in? Everyone shouted Hosanna to the Son of David, and laid palm branches in his path. Some say he is the promised Messiah, and I think so too." said Ben.

Joshua had such a busy day his head was whirling. Suddenly he realized how late it was getting. When he found his father, he was still talking with the scribes, Pharisees, Sadducees and priests. They all looked very serious.

Joshua was bursting to tell his father the good news about Old Ben, and how Jesus had healed him; but he could see his father was far too preoccupied to listen. When they reached home, his mother was bustling about preparing the dinner and could not listen either.

"Later," she assured him, "but not now, Josh."

Soon their home was filled with guests. Among them was Caiaphas, the high priest. It was unusually quiet for such a festive night. Joshua asked the four traditional Passover questions. He was well prepared for his bar mitzvah and could have easily answered all of the questions very well himself.

Now was his chance. "I'll tell you why tonight is special," he blurted out. "My friend, Old Ben, isn't blind any more. Jesus of Nazareth healed him."

"I'll have no more of that talk, Son," shouted his father angrily. "He's causing a lot of trouble at the temple, I hear."

Caiaphas seemed uncomfortable and soon excused himself. "I have much work to do yet," he said. The other guests followed.

Meanwhile, Joshua could not understand why he was being sent to bed early on such an important night. He protested, "He's the Messiah, everyone says so. You'll see—Elijah will surely come tonight to announce him. Tonight is special. I will always remember tonight."

Joshua was not allowed to go to the temple the next day. Strangely enough, his father did not go either. He had not slept well all night. Maybe it was just too many rich foods the day before. But Joshua could see how his father's mind was troubled by the way he wrinkled his brow.

Neither father nor son spoke very much, but each time their eyes met, they sensed something special was going on. Joshua was not the type of boy to get excited for no reason. His father knew that. In spite of his apparent anger in front of Caiaphas, he could not forget the things his son had to say about Jesus. By afternoon a tremendous darkness came over the land. While a little frightening, there was a feeling of reassurance that all was in God's hands.

It was three days before they returned to the city of Jerusalem and heard the news that Jesus of Nazareth had been crucified and then had risen from the dead.

"Why do the people act so surprised?" asked Joshua. "Didn't they know something special happens at Passover, and Jesus is special? I knew that."

"I guess I knew it too," said his father as they walked home together. Their family would never be the same again.

SS1869

A VERY SPECIAL DONKEY

by Anne Evans

The little gray donkey hung his head and sighed. Why must he always be different from the rest?

Maybe it was because his mother told him he was special. "Some day," she said, shaking her wise old head, "something very special is going to happen to you. Don't be like the rest of the donkeys, hauling water and working in the fields. Keep yourself above the others. You're special. I know it. Mothers always know."

So Gray Donkey was very careful when he romped in the fields. He was careful to watch out for holes and roots so he wouldn't trip and break his legs. And he never, never rolled in the dust like the others, getting their coats all dusty and matted. No, his coat was always shiny and clean.

SS1869

"See how he thinks he's better than we are," scoffed the other donkeys. And they stayed away from him.

Gray Donkey was very sad. He knew he was different, but deep in his heart he wanted to be like the rest. He wanted to run and roll in the dust with them. He wanted to go to market with them and carry food and gay pots and jars.

But the man always looked at him, alone in the field, and said, "That donkey is just plain no good. I will take him to the market near Jerusalem and sell him. Maybe someone else will get some use out of him." And he flung a dirty blanket over Gray Donkey's back and tried to mount him.

"No, no," cried Gray Donkey. "You will never ride on my clean back with your dirty blanket." And he kicked up his heels and threw the man to the ground.

"Miserable animal," cried the man. "I'll ride you yet." And his rough hands grabbed Gray Donkey's neck and he threw his leg over Gray Donkey's back and again tried to ride him.

"No, no," cried Gray Donkey again. "You'll not ride on my back. I'm a very special donkey." And again he threw the man to the ground.

"I'll fix you," cried the angry man. And going over to a bush, he cut a stout branch. "Now we will see who is master," he said as he laid the whip on Gray Donkey's back. "Take that, and that," he shrieked as he beat the poor little animal. "I'll ride you yet, or I shall sell you."

Great tears rolled down Gray Donkey's cheeks, and his back bled where the man had beaten him. But Gray Donkey shook his head and said, "No, you will not ride me. I am a very special donkey." And each time the man tried to ride him, Gray Donkey threw him to the ground.

Gray Donkey was very sad. "What is the matter with me?" he asked his mother. "I want to be like the others, but I seem to do everything wrong. And now the man is going to sell me."

"Remember," said his mother, "you are a very special donkey and there is a reason for everything. Some day you'll know."

 SS1869

But Gray Donkey remained unhappy, and he walked beside the man as he took him to market.

"I'll sell this worthless creature to some fool who thinks he can tame him," said the man as he trudged along the dusty road. The hot sun beat down upon him, making him feel mean and ugly. "I walk, when I should be riding this useless beast," he sputtered, and gave Gray Donkey a kick with his boot.

And on they went, until they came to where two roads met on the edge of town.

"Worthless beast," said the man, "we will rest here for a while," And tying Gray Donkey to a post, the man sat down to rest under a tree.

Meanwhile, in nearby Bethany, Jesus and his disciples were making ready to come to Jerusalem for the Passover festival.

"Go to the edge of town," said Jesus, "and there you will find a donkey that has never been ridden. Untie him and bring him back to me so that I may ride him into Jerusalem."

"But, Master," said the disciples, "how will we know which donkey you mean. All donkeys have been ridden some time or other."

Jesus heaved a patient sigh. "Go," he said. "It will be a very special donkey. You will know. And if anyone asks you why you want him, tell them the Lord hath need of him."

And so two of the disciples headed for Jerusalem to find the donkey that Jesus wanted.

It was a long walk for them, and the sun was hot. Off in the distance they could see a spot where two roads met. A group of people had gathered.

"Let us see what is happening," said the disciples. And they came upon the crowd that was gathered around a little gray donkey.

 SS1869

"I will give you two pieces of silver, and no more," said a young man as he stepped forward and took the rope that tied Gray Donkey. "But first I must try him." And he started to climb upon Gray Donkey's back.

"No, no," brayed Gray Donkey. "You cannot ride me." And he threw the young man to the ground.

"What is the matter with this animal?" asked the young man as he picked himself up and dusted himself off. "Has this animal never been ridden?"

The man just shook his head.

"Well, I'll ride him," said the young man in a determined voice. "I'll show him who is master. But first I'll give him a taste of the whip." And he drew forth his whip and began to beat Gray Donkey.

"No! No!" cried the disciples as they stepped forward and took the whip from the young man. "The Lord has need of this donkey. It is a very special animal." And they took the rope from the young man's hand and led Gray Donkey to Jesus.

"Master," they said, "here is the donkey that has never been ridden."

Jesus put his hands on Gray Donkey's nose and patted him. How gentle his hands felt to Gray Donkey, and how his voice filled with love as he spoke to the little animal. Gray Donkey knew then that his moment had come.

He stood still, ever so still, as the disciples put their robes over him and Jesus climbed upon his back and rode into Jerusalem.

"Hosanna! Hosanna!" cried the crowd that gathered to see Jesus. "Hosanna!" they cried again. "Blessed is he that cometh in the name of the Lord."

Soon people were gathering palms to throw in the path of Jesus so he would not ride through the dirt and dust. And some were so happy to see their Savior that they stripped off their cloaks and threw them in the path. And Jesus entered into Jerusalem upon the back of a very proud and happy donkey.

Now Gray Donkey knew why he was so special—he had a very special duty to perform for a very special person—the Lord Jesus.

SS1869

ISAAC AND THE PARADE

by K. H. Munn

He heard the rooster crow loudly in the yard, and he thought grumpily of how nice it would be when they would have him for dinner and silence forever his raucous greetings to the dawn. Isaac looked out the window and saw that, if anything, the rooster had been a little late with his greeting that morning. The sun was already streaming in, showing Isaac every small piece of dust that floated in the air.

"Isaac," his mother's voice echoed in the stairway, "breakfast is on the table, come on down here."

SS1869

So Isaac rubbed his fist into his dark brown eyes, trying to wipe away the sleep, then ran his fingers through his hair—black as the bottom of his mother's cooking pots—in an effort to look neater for his family. He then bounded out of bed; he was ten years old and full of energy. He shrugged into his tunic, which was an ankle-length shirt-like item of clothing worn probably because it was so nice and cool in a hot climate, and bounced down the stairs. When he got to the main room, he saw that his parents and sisters were already seated at the table, waiting for him.

Isaac walked to his chair, poking his sister Esther as he passed, and sat down. Immediately his father said the prayer of thanksgiving to the one God of Israel for the food and just about every other blessing that he could think of. Isaac peeked at his family throughout the prayer, thinking to himself that his father was, as usual, certainly thankful.

When his father had finally finished, Isaac's mother handed him his breakfast of sliced tomatoes and cucumbers, served with flat bread—which was a kind of pancake-like thing—much like the tortilla that Mexican people eat today.

Isaac was enjoying the last of his breakfast when his father spoke again, for the first time since the long prayer. "Last night when I was sitting with the men in the courtyard near the well, (Isaac looked at the ceiling impatiently) Samuel, the shoemaker, told me he had heard a rumor that a messiah is coming to Jerusalem today. He's going to make his triumphal entry into the city." Isaac knew that *messiah* meant the same thing that *great ruler*, *powerful leader* and *king*, all rolled together, mean today. He also knew, because the residents of Jerusalem spoke Greek in those days, that *christ* meant the same thing in Greek as *messiah* did in Hebrew.

"He's coming to save our people," Isaac's father went on. "He must be a great warrior! Warriors always ride powerful war horses, you know. It should be a really fine parade with the Messiah leading his army into the city on a beautiful Arabian stallion. Samuel says his name is Jesus."

This made Isaac happy. He loved a fine parade and he guessed that it was good, as well, that the Messiah was going to save his people, though he *did* wonder, just a little, what he was going to save them from.

So, after wolfing down the remains of his meal, Isaac ran into the street, poking again at his beautiful older sister Esther as he passed her on the way. He enjoyed seeing girls angry, and nothing made Esther angrier than being poked by her younger brother.

Isaac hung around in the street for a while, throwing stones at his friends' houses to hurry them up, until they finally emerged. Some of their fathers emerged too, to look at the damage Isaac had done to their mud-walled homes and yell at Isaac in anger. Isaac ran and hid in the alley. It was scary, but thrilling as well, to have the men angry at him—kind of like how modern kids feel about a monster movie.

After the fathers had all gone to work or back into their damaged homes, Isaac joined his friends in the street, and they talked over the big parade to come. Jacob, the kid that lived across the street,

Shining Star Publications, Copyright © 1989, A division of Good Apple, Inc.

SS1869

said that when warriors entered a city people always waved palm branches and laid them in the street for the warrior to ride over. The kids all liked the idea, so they ran off to cut the palm fronds they knew of, the ones that mothers carefully tended in their yards.

It wasn't long until the kids were all gathered back in the street, each with a big bundle of palm fronds, to the sound of angry women yelling at them from their doorways. Most of the kids had done their palm frond cutting in neighbors' yards, not their own; the same way kids today pick flowers. Isaac and his friends just shrugged and hoped their mothers wouldn't find out.

Isaac was sorry he had done this, but he went along when the rest of the kids left. They all went off, running and socking at each other as ten-year-olds do, towards the gate to the city. They didn't know when the parade was to start, but they wanted to be there for the excitement.

As things sometimes happen, it wasn't long at all until someone shouted, "Here comes the Messiah!" People ran out of nearby houses, carrying their own palm fronds, and gathered for the big show.

Suddenly he was there. A youngish-looking man with a kindly but not at all handsome face, mostly covered by a short black beard, came riding through the city gate on a young donkey that barely looked strong enough to hold him up. One of the small group of people straggling along behind him shouted, "The Messiah is here, our great and holy King!"

Oh well, thought Isaac, he's only riding a donkey, but if this is the Messiah . . . . And he did as kids had been doing at parades for centuries before him and have done for all the centuries since.

He shouted loudly in greeting. "Hey, Messiah, hey Jesus. Hi." Then he waved his palm fronds and started throwing them onto the street in front of the young man on the donkey.

The young man waved and winked at Isaac as he approached, then said to him, "You expected a war horse, didn't you, Isaac?" And Isaac nodded his head. Then Jesus said, with a small smile, "I know, I'm not the kind of messiah the people expected. They expected a warrior and I'm the Prince of Peace." Then Isaac thought he saw the young man's eyes fill with tears. "I've come to die,"

he said. "My father sent me as the final sacrifice for the forgiveness of the sins of mankind." Then he smiled again and patted Isaac on the shoulder. "They must come in a childlike way to be accepted," he said, then continued, "A great man will write something about me someday that millions of children all over the world will memorize and remember, even as adults. It will be called John 3:16, and will go like this: "For God so loved the world that he gave his only begotten son, that whosoever believeth on him shall not perish, but have everlasting life." Then He smiled again, as the tears escaped from His eyes and rolled down His cheeks. "I don't want people to kill me, I love them," he said. Then He patted Isaac again and rode off on His little donkey, calling back over His shoulder, "Good-bye for now, Isaac."

Just then Isaac felt an arm encircle his waist and looked to see who it belonged to. It was his beautiful sister, Esther, standing there by him. As they watched Jesus ride away they cried too, unashamed, neither knowing whether they were tears of sorrow or joy.

SS1869

THE DONKEY

by Marion Schoeberlein

Zarian followed Jesus as he rode Zarian's little donkey, Ulysses, through the streets of Jerusalem.

It was a perfect morning world—a Sunday filled with children like himself and games and shouting.

He had heard many stories about Jesus—about His healing powers and His miracles. Father says He is becoming a threat and a danger to the Pharisees and Scribes, he thought, and they have a plot against Him. But if this was true, why did He pick on a little donkey to ride? A donkey could not keep him from death anymore than he could keep the people from spreading palm branches in His path.

"Hosanna!" the people cried. "Blessed is He that cometh in the name of the Lord!"

Zarian hoped that none of the spies for the Sanhedrin heard the chant. They would be very jealous!

The little donkey with the shiny, beige coat stopped while a woman put a blue blanket on his back and a blue necklace around his neck.

This is a day for a donkey to dream about, Zarian thought, hardly believing his eyes. The little animal must be living out a poem, just as Zarian was.

The donkey and Jesus stopped at a broken stone wall to rest. Bouquets of palm leaves were everywhere.

I would not have shared him with anyone but the Master, Zarian thought. He is all I have. It was true. Zarian's mother was a poor widow and the donkey had been given to him as a present from a neighbor.

I always knew there was something special about my donkey, he thought, but I never knew that Jesus and His disciples would ask me for him.

It was easy to see that Jesus was not a burden for the animal to carry.

He must be enjoying every moment, Zarian thought. This is his very first ride into Jerusalem.

There were whispers, though, in the crowd. Evil whispers. "Who does this man think he is? A king?" Zarian was sure it must be some of the Sanhedrin's spies.

Jesus did not look afraid, though. He looked very calm and very happy. He held out His hands to the children. He smiled at the people. Then He stopped and motioned to Zarian. At last the ride was over and he could take his donkey home.

He ran quickly to the place where Jesus had tied the animal. "Oh, Ulysses, I am so glad you are safe!" he cried, hugging the donkey. Zarian had named him Ulysses because he thought it would be a good name for a donkey.

Jesus was now walking the streets of Jerusalem with His disciples. The people were still shouting His praises.

It was a long, slow journey going home. Zarian and the donkey walked silently on the now deserted roads.

"I will always remember this day," Zarian told the donkey, "and I have you to thank for it. Just imagine, riding with Jesus. Many say He is the Son of God. Do you think He is?"

Then a strange thing happened. Ulysses made a loud, snorting noise, almost as if he were a horse.

He looked at Zarian out of beady brown eyes.

I think he means yes, Zarian thought. Even an animal, even a donkey, knew after today that Jesus was the King of Kings!

SS1869

THE LAST SUPPER

by Anne Evans

It was a dark, narrow alley and Wee Mouse crouched in a doorway. There was no moon that night. Nearby, two men were whispering. Wee Mouse strained her ears to hear what they were saying.

"How will we know which one he is?" asked the older man.

"I will give you a sign," said the other man as he glanced over his shoulder to make sure no one heard him. "I will throw my arms around him and kiss him. By that you will know him."

"Good," said the older man. "We will capture him when there isn't a crowd around to protect him." And reaching into the folds of his robe he brought out a leather purse, saying, "Here, take this, Judas. It is thirty pieces of silver for what you will do. It will be well worth it when we capture this man who claims to be a savior. This man who calls himself King of the Jews."

Judas took the thirty pieces of silver and hurried into the shadows.

"What does this mean?" said Wee Mouse to herself. "They must be talking about Jesus." But why would Judas betray Jesus? Judas was a disciple. He was supposed to love Jesus. What terrible thing would happen to Jesus if wicked people captured him?

Wee Mouse returned to her nest, her head bent low in sadness. Someone must tell Jesus that Judas and some wicked men were plotting to destroy him. But who would tell him? Certainly not his enemies, and his followers didn't know about Judas' betrayal. And surely no one would pay any attention to a tiny mouse.

Wee Mouse was very upset. She thought about the strange conversation until she fell asleep, and when she awoke she hurried up the stairs to a large room where a table was being set for the Passover feast. Many crumbs would fall on the floor, and Wee Mouse would have a feast of her own.

She looked about the room. Thirteen chairs were placed around a table spread with a huge roast of lamb surrounded by nuts and raisins and many bitter-tasting herbs. At each plate was a loaf of bread and a goblet for wine.

Wee Mouse counted the chairs again. Thirteen! "Why, that must be for Jesus and His Twelve Disciples," she squeaked. "He's coming here to this very room." Then she thought for a moment and said, "And Judas will be here too. How dare he!"

She crept under the table and waited. She thought of Judas' plan to betray Jesus. Suddenly there was a crowd of people at the door, and Jesus and his disciples came in and sat at the table. How tired Jesus look-

SS1869

ed; his shoulders drooped with weariness.

A stillness hung over the room. Jesus looked at his disciples and said, "My followers, this will be my last supper with you." No one felt like eating after they heard Jesus' words.

"Do not feel badly," said Jesus, his voice filled with love. "I must leave you, for I go to my Father in heaven. But a new commandment I give unto you that you love one another even as I have loved you."

"But we do love one another," cried Thomas, "even as we love you."

A note of sadness crept into Jesus' voice as he heaved a great sigh and replied, "Truly, truly, I say unto you, that one of you will betray me."

"He knows! He knows!" cried Wee Mouse from under the table. But Wee Mouse's squeak was drowned out by the surprise in the disciples' voices.

"Is it I? Is it I?" each disciple cried out. But Judas remained silent, his face pale with fear.

Then John looked at Matthew, suspicion darkening his face as he said, "Surely it cannot be you, Matthew, my friend."

"I?" replied Matthew. "I thought it was you."

And Peter said to Andrew, "Tell me it isn't you. I could never believe such a thing of you." And the disciples looked at each other, distrust showing in their faces. Now, instead of love for one another, there was suspicion and doubt.

"No! No!" squeaked Wee Mouse as she ran from one to the other. "Stop doubting each other. Have faith in those you love. It isn't right for disciples to feel this way about each other. Jesus taught you to love."

Jesus shook his head in sadness. "Come, eat," he said. But the disciples only picked at their food. No one felt like eating, especially Judas. He just stared down at his plate, his shoulders slumped and his toes curled in a tight knot.

Wee Mouse wondered what Judas would do. She looked at all the crumbs that had fallen on the floor. Here was a feast for her. She could even take some of the food back to her nest, but she didn't feel like eating either. Her thoughts were on Judas.

Judas remained silent. He knew he would still betray Jesus, but his guilty conscience made him ask in a voice scarcely above a whisper, "Is it I, Master?" And his fingers curled around the thirty pieces of silver.

SS1869

"Thou hast spoken," answered Jesus. "Yes, it is you. Do what you must and do it quickly. And Judas left the room.

"Jesus knew all the time that it was Judas," said Wee Mouse to herself, "and yet he still loved Judas enough to ask him to come to his last supper."

Wee Mouse's heart swelled with love for Jesus. If only she could comfort him.

The disciples watched Judas leave the room. Then John turned to Matthew, his voice filled with love, "Forgive me, dear friend, for doubting you," he said. "I didn't know it was Judas."

"Nor I," replied Matthew. And the disciples all turned to each other and begged forgiveness. Again, there was love and trust among them.

The disciples settled down and turned their eyes to Jesus. And Jesus took a loaf of bread from the table and slowly broke it into small pieces. Wee Mouse watched and hoped there would be some crumbs left for her.

Jesus looked at his disciples, and one by one he gave each a bit of the bread, saying, "Take this bread and eat it, for this bread is my body which I give for you." And the disciples ate the bread and thought of Jesus' words.

Then Jesus poured a cup of wine and blessed it and passed it to the disciples. His voice was sad as he said, "Drink this, my followers; for this cup of wine is my blood, which I shall shed for you so you may be saved from your sins." And each disciple took the cup and drank, knowing that Jesus would give his life for them.

The room was very still. No one spoke. Wee Mouse was still. Her mind was in a whirl.

It is a time to be sad, she thought half aloud, but we must think about what Jesus said. He said he was going to his heavenly Father. There he will find peace and happiness. We must be happy for him.

And Wee Mouse gathered up the crumbs that had fallen on the floor and ate them, for she knew that Jesus had blessed them. And she, too, was blessed.

Shining Star Publications, Copyright © 1989, A division of Good Apple, Inc.   SS1869

THE DAY THE DONKEY CRIED
by Katherine D. M. Marko

He was an old donkey, much older than any of the others who stood, awkward and uneasy, beneath the olive trees. From the grove they could look up at the place called Golgotha. He had seen many processions to this hill where men who broke the law were crucified.

But, this crucifixion, he felt, would be different from all others. This day would be set apart for always.

A huge sigh rose from his throat, and his head hung low. He had lived too long, he told himself, so long that the others simply called him the Old One. Many times he had felt he should die and be out of the way. Today he wished it most.

His joints were stiff and sore. He could no longer carry a burden or do a day's work. And now there came an empty feeling to add to his sense of uselessness.

He had followed the other donkeys through the streets of Jerusalem and out from the city behind the crowd. It had been difficult to keep up with the younger donkeys.

One of them, boastful and sneering, called back, "Hurry, Old One, or you will miss everything."

The Old One wanted to say that this was not a festival, but he kept silent and plodded on. The dust, churned up by so many feet, rested on his straggly mane, his ears and his long face. It was good to reach the shade of the olive trees.

The pound-pound-pound of the hammer had ceased, but the crosses were being raised; today there were three. But the Old One looked only at the center cross on which hung a man named Christ, bleeding and crowned with thorns. This was the God-Man whom many jeered at and called a false Messiah. But all wondered and spoke about Him.

In the crowd of curious onlookers, mockers and Roman soldiers there were a few sad, heartbroken people who loved and revered Christ.

As they watched, the younger donkeys were silent for the most part, except for the boastful one. He chattered on as though he knew much more than the others. "The two on the outer crosses are thieves," he brayed. "Common thieves."

"Braggart!" the Old One muttered. He was not impressed. Instead he looked at one other donkey who stood apart from the group, alone and grief-stricken. The Old One wished he could go and lay his face against the bowed head of this lonely, sad donkey. But he knew this would only bring more sneering talk from the braggart.

Whenever a moan came from the cross in the center, the Old One looked quickly at Christ. One of the thieves was silent and sorrowful.

SS1869

The other one was loud and surly. "If you are God," he called to Christ, "save yourself and me."

But when the God-Man spoke or cried out, the words came as from afar—from another world. No voice ever sounded like that before. The Old One bowed his head and cried.

Time passed so slowly, it seemed to stand still. The Roman soldiers had divided all the belongings of the condemned men except for the robe of Christ. Each seemed to like it and want it, so they drew lots. Their actions and talk were so cold and ruthless, the Old One did not watch to see who won.

Separated from the curious onlookers there stood a little group of women, weeping. One, in a cloak of blue, had the most beautiful eyes the Old One had ever seen. Her lovely, slender hands stretched out and upward each time the God-Man cried out; for He was her son.

Whenever there was laughter or a rough shout from the crowd, the Old One wanted to lower his head and butt the offenders hard. He wanted to hurt them, to scatter them. But he could only stand still and cry, helpless while he watched this terrible thing.

 SS1869

It seemed he had been crying for hours. The other donkeys were all looking at him now. To be noticed was something new. Usually he was just one of the crowd, to whom no one paid any attention. Their silent stares left him flustered for a moment. Then the braggart spoke. "Why do you cry so long, Old One?" The question was cruel. "You are not like the rest of us." Here the braggart nodded toward the sad, lonely donkey. "He carried the Crucified One into Jerusalem over the palms strewn on the road. We walked alongside, bearing the noted ones of the city." He puffed with pride. "You have no such reason."

"Oh, but I do, I do." The Old One could not keep the anguish from his reply. "Long ago over another road I carried a lady to the little town of Bethlehem." His sad, wet eyes turned to the cluster of weeping women. "She stands there beneath the cross."

The braggart's head jerked, and he was silent.

Yes, the Old One thought, it WAS a long time ago. But no matter how many others he had carried since, he would always remember her.

Suddenly the sun darkened. Thunder sounded and lightning streaked the skies. The wind whipped savagely as though to beat down all those responsible for this mockery of justice.

Many in the crowd grew frightened and began to leave. Some clutched others, some went alone—all hurrying, running while the earth trembled under their feet.

The Old One looked up again. At last it was over. The great God-Man was dead. The crude, mocking sign of INRI on His cross was tattered and flapping in the angry winds.

A centurion went toward the center cross. Watching him, the Old One was filled with rage. But his rage faded immediately when he heard the centurion admit, "He is indeed the Son of God."

A rustle was heard among the few remaining who were loyal to Christ. A man named Joseph from Arimathaea was going toward the cross. There he directed the men to take down the body of Christ.

Through his tears the Old One watched their movements until they placed Christ in the arms of the lady. Then a change gripped him and he felt as through he were dreaming. The sights and sounds of Golgotha were fading away, returning and fading away again. A beautiful peace seemed to wrap around him. The half darkness made him think of a calm night long ago. The sky then was a dome of deep, dark blue, and breaking through it was one great, golden star.

A calm sky for the God-Man's coming, a stormy one for His death, the Old One thought; and his own eyes had looked upon both. At last it made sense to have lived so long.

Slowly the wind lessened, the thunder hushed and the quaking of the earth ceased.

The Old One's breath was becoming difficult now. His creaky, stiff joints were giving out, but he would bend his knee a last time in silent salute to the God-Man. As he knelt shakily, his tears rolled into the dust and were swept away across the hill.

Then as the whole scene faded from his sight, he toppled over on his side. While he still had his sense of hearing, he heard the braggart's voice, filled with amazement say, "Look—the Old One's feet! They look as if they were shod with gold."

Then the Old One stretched out and lay still.

SS1869

CHORAL READINGS

Shining Star Publications, Copyright © 1989, A division of Good Apple, Inc.   SS1869

CHORAL READING TIPS

Choral speaking, as a vocal activity, dates back five hundred years before the birth of Christ. In Greek drama, the odes were recited or chanted with accompanying body movements. The revival of choral reading is receiving wide acceptance in the modern classroom. Its value as a form of artistic expression has innumerable benefits. It is fun and it certainly increases the love of poetry. It helps the timid to develop, while restraining the aggressive. It establishes confidence within the group. Greatest of all, it improves speech. If you have been wanting to begin a speaking choir, don't hesitate. The selections found on the following pages will provide you with entertainment and an opportunity to advance individuals through group participation.

The organization is not difficult, and even the smallest group can enjoy the fun that comes from speaking together. A choir may include as few as eight, or a hundred or more. The leader is an important part of the organization. The leader should have a sense of rhythm and some knowledge of interpretation.

There are many ways to present choral readings:

1. The group (if large enough) may be divided into Choir 1 and Choir 2, each speaking certain assigned parts, then the entire group speaking on Chorus. Short poems are best suited to this type.
2. Line-a-Child is more difficult, as the timing must be perfect from one person to the next.
3. Part-speaking is used when different groups take parts of the selection.
4. Solo and Chorus uses various members of the group speaking certain lines and then they join together on the chorus. This can be a recitation format and works well with small children.
5. Unison Speaking is the most difficult type of choral reading. This means that the entire group speaks as one person. This requires perfect timing, balance, phrasing and harmony in inflection. Not to be performed in sing-song fashion!

The standard procedure in presentation of choral selections is as follows:

1. The leader recites the selection as it should be presented. Then it is repeated line by line to see if the meaning is grasped by the group.
2. The leader recites the selection again, having the group read along silently, if they are of reading age. If not, have them repeat each line orally. Encourage wide-open mouth movements.
3. Solo parts may be assigned here (if desired).
4. Memorization is required before proceeding if this is to be a presentation before an audience. Give each child a copy of the readings you will be performing.

Staging may take various forms:

1. Choir may be placed in rows on risers (if group is large) with arms at sides. If solo parts have been assigned, place high voices on the left, medium in the center and low on the right. Small children do not have enough variance in voice range for the division to be based on voice tone.
2. With a smaller group, have choir stand shoulder to shoulder with arms behind them. Each speaker steps forward, presents his/her selection and then steps back into place.

It is advisable for the leader to stand before the group (as with a singing choir) and direct. All eyes should stay fixed on the director who speaks the words, with all facial expressions, silently. This helps keep the group together. However, if the group is small and each person is to speak alone, the director may be seated in front and stand only when the entire group speaks in unison. HAPPY DIRECTING! IT'S GREAT FUN!

SS1869

FROM TEARS TO JOY

by Marilyn Senterfitt

This choral reading will enable children to have a feeling for the great sadness on the day of the Crucifixion and the unbounding joy on the day of Resurrection.

(Jesus stands facing audience with hands folded.)

BOYS AND GIRLS: It is a day of great sadness. Our Master has been arrested.

PETER: They took Him before the Sanhedrin and Herod and Pilate.

BOYS AND GIRLS: He was treated so unfairly.

BOYS: He was beaten and mocked.

GIRLS: It is a day of great sadness. Our Master has been abused.

PETER: Pilate wanted to release Him but the crowd cried . . .

BOYS AND GIRLS: Crucify Him! Crucify Him!

JOHN: He was taken to Golgotha, that terrible place of death.

BOYS AND GIRLS: Oh pain! Oh sorrow! Our Master has been nailed to a cruel cross.

(Jesus holds out arms as if nailed to a cross.)

JOHN: The soldiers gambled for His robe. He looked down from the cross and said . . .

JESUS: Father, forgive them; they do not know what they are doing.

GIRLS: Our hearts are breaking. We cannot endure this sorrow.

MARY: Two thieves were crucified with my Son. Jesus spoke to one of them.

JESUS: Indeed, I promise you, today you will be with me in paradise.

BOYS AND GIRLS: He suffers so. We cannot bear to see His pain. It is a day of unbearable sadness. Our Master is dying.

MARY: I heard His last words. My beloved Son said . . .

JESUS: Father, into your hands I commit my spirit.

(Jesus bows head with arms still outstretched.)

SS1869

BOYS AND GIRLS: Never have we known such despair. He is gone. Our Master is dead.

(Two boys step forward and put their hands under Jesus' arms as if lifting Him from the cross. Jesus kneels to the floor with head bowed low.)

TWO BOYS: We have a terrible task to perform. We must bury our dead Master.

GIRLS: There is not even time to prepare the body. We are drowning in our tears.

(Two boys return to choir.)

BOYS: Friday evening was filled with gloom. We hid in the upper room. We, too, could be arrested or killed.

GIRLS: All day Saturday we wanted to go to the tomb. How can He be gone? Our souls are in torment.

BOYS AND GIRLS: There has never been such a time of sadness. How will we go on without Him?

GIRLS: The sun arose. Now we could go to the tomb.

MARY MAGDALENE: When we arrived in the garden the ground began to shake.

GIRLS: It was an earthquake!

JOANNA: We hurried to the tomb. The stone had been rolled away and an angel sat upon it!

SALOME: The angel said he knew we were looking for Jesus, who was crucified; but He was not there. For He had risen, just as He said He would.

GIRLS: Joy! Rejoice! Our Master is alive!

MARY MAGDALENE: I alone did not believe. I waited for a moment outside the tomb. Someone came up to me. I thought it was the gardener. He spoke . . .

JESUS: Woman, why are you weeping? Who are you looking for?

MARY MAGDALENE: I asked the man if he knew where my Master's body had been taken. He only said . . .

JESUS: Mary.

MARY MAGDALENE: It was my Master! He truly was alive!

GIRLS: Joy! Rejoice! Our Master has risen from the dead. We must tell the others!

PETER: The women say He lives. Can it be?

JOHN: Peter and I ran to the tomb. It was empty. Is our Master alive?

GIRLS: Some say He lives.

BOYS: Some say they are not sure. We have locked the doors. We don't know what else to do.

BOYS AND GIRLS: Then suddenly He was among us!

JESUS: Peace be with you. As the Father sent me, so am I sending you. Go out to the whole world; proclaim the Good News to all creation.

(Everyone gathers around Jesus. Their faces show the joy they feel as they say with great emphasis . . .)

BOYS AND GIRLS: Praise God! Our Master lives! Praise God! Our Lord and Saviour lives now and forevermore!

SS1869

LIFE, LIFE, LIFE

by Edith E. Cutting

Speaker (*Holds out closed hands.*)

Here is a stone, and here is a seed.
What is the difference between them indeed?

Chorus: (*Firmly*) Life, life, life!

Speaker: (*Looks in each hand.*)

Each one is little and hard and round.
I put each one in a hole in the ground. (*Bends over and "plants" each, then stands up again.*)

Chorus: (*Softly*) Life, life, life!

Speaker: (*Bends down to look where stone was planted.*)

The stone doesn't change; it's always a stone.
It stays there, still hard and dead and alone.

Chorus: (*Sadly*) No life, no life, no life.

Speaker: (*Looks where seed was planted and mimes growing plant with upstretching arms and smiling, lifted face.*)

The seed sends out a stem and a root.
It turns into green leaves and flowers and fruit.

Chorus: (*Joyously*) Life, life, life!

Speaker: Like the empty tomb, the seed is gone,
But just like Jesus, its life goes on.

Chorus: (*Joyously*) Life, life, life!

EASTER MORNING

by Edith E. Cutting

1st half of group: Out of the darkness
2nd half: comes the light.
1st: Out of our blindness
2nd: comes new sight.
1st: Out of the tomb
2nd: comes the living Lord.
1st: Out of His life
2nd: comes the living Word.
Unison: JESUS!

A DUET FOR EASTER

by Edith E. Cutting

1st speaker: You wouldn't see starlight
2nd speaker: Without the night.
1st: You wouldn't see moonglow
2nd: Without blackness below.
1st: You wouldn't see sunrise
2nd: Without midnight skies,
1st: Or know Easter in bloom
2nd: Without Friday's dark tomb.

HOSANNA!

by Kay Erlandson

". . . Hosanna! Blessed is he who comes in the name
of the Lord!" 　　　　　　　　　　　Mark 11:9 NIV

1st speaker:　He is coming.
2nd speaker:　Yes, that is him.
3rd speaker:　But he is riding on a donkey.
　　　　　　　Are you sure we are to worship him?

3rd speaker:　He is coming.
1st speaker:　Yes, I see him.
2nd speaker:　He is not wearing a robe or crown.
All together:　Is this the King we have come to praise?

1st speaker:　He is coming.
2nd speaker:　Lay down your palm branches.
3rd speaker:　Lay down your garments.
　　　　　　　Make his path comfortable.

1st speaker:　He is coming.
　　　　　　　Praise him.
2nd speaker:　Hosanna, Hosanna!
　　　　　　　Praise the King!

1st speaker:　Will he come again?
2nd speaker:　Yes! He will return one day.
All together:　Then he will truly be King forever!
　　　　　　　Hosanna!

SS1869

ESPECIALLY FOR PRESCHOOLERS

SPRINGTIME
by Helen Kitchell Evans

Boy 1: Don't you think I am BRAVE
To announce that Spring is here?

Boy 2: Sometimes the blustery winds blow
(*Slower*)
But still we have good cheer.

Girl 1: What if it's cold and chilly—
The warm days soon will start;

Girl 2: Besides—it's almost Springtime
When you keep a happy heart.

HE WILL HELP
by Helen Kitchell Evans

Boys: Jesus wants to help us
On Easter and each day;

Girls: If we will be very quiet
We can hear what He has to say.

All together: Shhhhhhhhhhhhhhhhhhhhhhhhhhh.

LITTLE THINGS
by Helen Kitchell Evans

Little things make the world go 'round—
At least I have been told.
So that is why I am so sure
I am worth my weight in gold!
(*Speak slowly and bring out last line very slowly.*)

LILIES PRESENTATION
by Helen Kitchell Evans

Child 1: These lovely flowers of Easter

Child 2: We hold in our hands today.

Child 3: We're going to present them.

All together: That's all we have to say.

(*They scatter all over the congregation handing out flowers to the elderly in a happy, joyful manner. The author used silk flowers, and it was a very pretty number in the program.*)

31

SS1869

EASTER BELLS

by Phyllis C. Michael

Ding-dong! Here's our song; Here is what we say:

"Ding-dong! Nothing's wrong; Jesus lives today."

(One primary child recites the verse, others sing the chorus. All may be dressed in bells made from cardboard covered with crepe paper, or each may carry a bell. The bells may be real or made from gold and silver paper.)

We are little Easter bells,
As you can plainly see;
We'd like to ring for Jesus,
True as we can be.

SS1869

HE LIVES

by Phyllis C. Michael

(Mary, mother of James and Salome, is designated here as Mary 1; Mary Magdalene is designated as Mary M.)

Scene I

Mary 1: (*Speaking to Mary Magdalene*) It's the first day of the week, Mary, don't you remember? Where are you going so early? And what do you have in your hands?

Mary M.: Yes, I remember. I'm going to the place where they put Jesus after He was crucified. I'm taking spices to put near His body to keep it better.

Girl 1: But you can't get in to do that!

Girl 2: There is a great big stone across the front of the place.

Boy 1: And the soldiers sealed the tomb shut!

Boy 2: The soldiers are guarding the tomb, too. Lots of them!

Girl 3: Why do they have to guard it?

All: (*Except individual speakers*)—Some folks say that His disciples may come and steal His body away. Some folks even say He will be alive again.

Girls: (*Except the two Marys*): How can that be?

Boys: Jesus can do anything He wants to do.

Girls: Anything?

Boys: Yes, ANYTHING!

Mary 1: OK, Mary, I'll go with you. We shall see.

Scene II

Mary M.: (*To angel*) Where is He? Where have you taken Him?

Angel: Do not be afraid, Mary. I know you are looking for Jesus who was crucified. He is not here. He is risen. Come and look for yourself at the place where He has been.

Mary M.: Oh, I remember! Jesus did say He would rise again after three days. It's true. It's TRUE!

Angel: Go quickly and tell His disciples that He is risen from the dead and that He is going to Galilee. He will meet them there.

Mary M.: Oh, I'm so happy. I'll hurry. His disciples will all want to know. They will be happy, too.

Chorus: (*In the background each of the following sentences shouted louder than the one before.*) He lives! Jesus LIVES! JESUS LIVES FOREVERMORE! HALLELUJAH! JESUS LIVES!

Note: Children may sing the first verse of "Jesus Arose," after Scene I and sing the second verse after Scene II. (See page 83.)

THE KING IS COMING

by Phyllis C. Michael

Scene I

(*Individuals who have special parts speak only as indicated and not with parts designated "All" or "Group."*)

All: (*Speaking to two disciples*) Where are you going, may we ask?

Two Disciples: We are going to the next town to get a donkey and a colt.

All: Why in the world would you want to get a donkey and a colt? What are you going to do with them?

Two Disciples: Jesus needs them. He told us to go and get them.

All: Just any donkey and colt you can find?

Two Disciples: No, a very special donkey, tied with a colt—right inside the nearby village.

All: But will the people let you take them?

Two Disciples: Yes! We will tell the people Jesus needs them.

All: OK! Go, if that is what Jesus wants you to do. Good luck!

Scene II

Child 1: The King is coming! The King is coming! (*Shouted*)

Group 1: Hosanna! Blessed be the King! (*Hands waved excitedly*)

Group 2: What King? Who are you talking about?

Group 1: Why Jesus, of course. He's God's own Son, the King we've been waiting for all these years.

Group 2: How do you know this Jesus is the King we've been waiting for?

Child 1 from Group 1: He teaches us all how to live and be happy.
            And He loves all of us children.

Child 2 from Group 1: He gives lots of people bread when there is only enough for two or three people.

Child 3 from Group 1: He makes sick people well.

Child 4 from Group 1: He makes blind people see again and deaf people hear.

Child 5 from Group 1: He even makes dead people alive again.

Child 1 from Group 2: You mean real dead people can walk and talk again?

Group 1: Yes! He made Lazarus alive again and Lazarus can go anywhere he wants to and say anything he wants to.

Group 2: (*In amazement*) You mean this Jesus is coming HERE?

Group 1: Yes! Oh, YES!

Child 1 from Group 1: Let's put our coats and some branches down so the donkey that Jesus is riding won't hurt its feet. (*All spread jackets or branches on floor.*)

Group 2: How do you know Jesus will be riding a donkey?

Group 1: The Bible says He will be coming like that this time.

Group 2: We believe you. We will watch and wait, too.

Child 2 from Group 1: THE KING IS COMING! THE KING IS COMING! (*Everyone shades eyes and turns to look.*)

*All: HOSANNA! BLESSED BE THE KING! HOSANNA IN THE HIGHEST! (*Children may make up their own phrases and shout them in unison or individually.*)

After Scene II, children may sing, "Hosanna!" (See page 84.)

SS1869

A PLACE IN HEAVEN

by Helen Kitchell Evans

1st speaker: Three days Jesus lay in the tomb.

2nd speaker: But then on Easter Day

3rd speaker: An angel came from heaven
And rolled the stone away.

Chorus:
Rolled the heavy stone away,
Set our Savior free
To return to heaven
To wait for you and for me.

1st speaker: "In my house are many mansions,"
He was heard to say.

2nd speaker: "I go to prepare a place for you.
You'll come to me some day."

Chorus:
How wonderful to know
That in heaven we'll have a place,
And be able to touch our Lord
And look upon His face.

A WONDERFUL THING

by Helen Kitchell Evans

Boys: Rainbows on stems
As we walk through the hills;
Golden trumpets we see
And bright daffodils.

Girls: Tulips stand proudly,
Announcing it's spring.
Isn't God's world
A wonderful thing?

SS1869

WORLD RENEWED
by Donna Colwell Rosser

1st speaker:
   Easter:

      Blooming daffodils and hyacinths,
      tulips promise, too.
      The first leaves bud on weeping willow:
      sky, a mild spring blue.

2nd speaker:
   Easter:

      Robin song is heard again.
      Children go out to play.
      Night is shortening just a bit,
      longer lasts the day.

3rd speaker:
   Easter:

      The world renews itself at this time
      and, lowly now, do we
      acknowledge that Christ, three days gone,
      arose triumphantly.

EASTER SPEAKS
by Helen Kitchell Evans

1st speaker:
   Easter speaks through birds and flowers,

2nd speaker:
   Through budding trees and springtime showers;

3rd speaker:
   Through Christian music as souls rejoice,

4th speaker:
   Filling churches with joyful voice.

1st speaker:
   Easter speaks through children who love

2nd speaker:
   And talk of the Father in heaven above.

3rd speaker:
   Easter speaks in tones loud and clear,

4th speaker:
   Bringing happiness to last all year.

Note: The song, "In Our Hearts," works well with these choral readings. (See page 87.)

A PSALM OF PRAISE

by Marilyn Senterfitt

This choral reading will give children an opportunity to praise God, play an instrument and learn Psalm 100!

INSTRUMENTS: Rattler—Provide aluminum pie tins and six to ten bottle caps for each child. Using a large nail or hole puncher, place holes evenly around tin and in caps. Pass out short lengths of yarn and instruct the children to tie caps to the tin.

Jingler—Give each child a coat hanger. They may be wrapped with yarn for more color. Provide small bells. Using yarn of different lengths, have children attach bells to the hanger.

PREPARATION: Have boys stand to left and girls to right. A child will stand center front holding a world globe. Be sure there are an equal number of rattlers and jinglers among the children.

Boys and Girls: "Make a joyful noise unto the Lord, all ye lands.
(*Child with globe steps forward. All children shout "Hosanna! Hosanna!" Child places globe on small table and steps back.*)

Boys and Girls: Serve the Lord with gladness: come before his presence with singing.
(*While shaking instruments children sing Hosanna!*) (See page 84.)

Boys: Know ye that the Lord he is God;

Girls: it is he that hath made us, and not we ourselves;

Boys: we are his people,

Girls: and the sheep of his pasture.

Boys: Enter into his gates with thanksgiving, and into his courts with praise:

be thankful unto him, and bless his name.

Girls: (*While shaking instruments, children may sing, "Blessed Is He."*)
(See page 86.)

Boys: For the Lord is good;

Girls: his mercy is everlasting;

and his truth endureth to all generations."

Boys and Girls: (*Children enthusiastically shake instruments.*)

   SS1869

HERALDS OF EASTER

by Helen Kitchell Evans

Child 1:

Easter is a time for joy,
All the earth seems new;
Flowers and birds and everything,
All nature speaks to you.

Easter is a time for praise
To our Lord who arose this day;
A time for songs of joy,
For the stone was rolled away.

Easter heralds springtime,
The end of winter and snow;
The swelling buds on trees
And daffodils all aglow.

Child 2:

Easter enters every church,
And sits in every pew;

Look around this morning;
Is Easter next to you?

Child 3:

Tulips tucked beneath the earth,
Now fill the springtime with their birth.
Covered long months beneath the snow,
Now they have begun to grow.
They sing of spring to passersby,
Singing praise to God on high.

Child 4:

Easter renews God's pledge to us.
Every year tells the wondrous story
Of how Jesus arose from the grave,
And now lives in heaven's glory.

Jesus lives in heaven's glory
And we can talk to Him there;
He listens to us carefully
When we say each prayer.

Child 5:

When sunshine fills the playground,
When the smell of lilacs is everywhere,
Then we know it's Easter;
The time for us to share.
Share again God's love for us.
How He died to save each one;
How God gave to the world
His only beloved Son.

Child 5 and 6:

Yes, we know it's Easter;
Happy day because He lives.
He's our wonderful, loving Savior;
Our Savior who forgives.

Note: The songs "Blessed Is He" and "In Our Hearts" work well with this choral reading. (See pages 86 and 87.)

 SS1869

WINTER'S PAST

by Helen Kitchell Evans

Chorus: Let us raise every voice,
Sing praise and rejoice!

Choir 1: God is beside us
To love and guide us;

Choir 2: His everlasting love is sure—
His love will endure!

Chorus: Let us raise every voice,
Sing praise and rejoice!

Choir 1: Birds are singing in flight.
They are free from the night.

Choir 2: There's a soft springtime breeze
Filtering through the green leaves;

Chorus: Let us raise every voice,
Sing praise and rejoice!

Choir 1: It's the dawning of day;
Darkness fades slowly away.

Choir 2: There is much to be done;

Chorus: Let us raise every voice,
Sing praise and rejoice.

This choral reading may be followed by singing of children's choir or entire congregation.

ARISE

by Helen Kitchell Evans

Choir 1: Come, let's take a walk today

Choir 2: Out across the hills.

Choir 1: Let's enjoy the sunshine

Choir 2: On all the daffodils.

Choir 1: Let's explore the wonder

Choir 2: Of God's lovely spring.

Choir 1: The earthly resurrection

Choir 2: Of every living thing.

Choir 1: Now the winter's past;

Choir 2: The cold days soon depart.

Solo: (*high*) Everything says, "Springtime!"

The flow of speaking from one choir to another should be smooth, never jerky. The words should always be spoken clearly and with expression— never allow the "sing-song" type of presentation. No matter how small the child, good clear speech can be taught so that no microphone is needed, no matter how large the church. Never say to the children, "Speak loudly." That defeats the purpose. Pauses in the proper places and clear enunciation are the keys to a good presentation.

THANK YOU, GOD, FOR SPRINGTIME

by Helen Kitchell Evans

First Child: All the earth is carpeted
By wildflowers in the spring;

Second Child: God seems nearer to me
When I see each newborn thing.

Third Child: There's the calf out in the field,

Fourth Child: The kittens in the shed;

Fifth Child: I have four brand-new puppies
That are eager to be fed.

Sixth Child: The bulbs begin to stir,
And the green peeks through the earth;

Seventh Child: Everything is bursting
With this new springtime birth.

All children: How we love the springtime!
Thank you, God above,
For all your springtime blessings
And your ever constant love.

This may be used, as written, for an exercise using seven children. However, it could also be used as a choral reading with any number of children. If used in this manner, change to the following: First Child—Choir 1, Second Child—Choir 2, Third Child—Choir 1, Fourth Child—Choir 2, Fifth Child—Solo, Sixth Child—Choir 1, Seventh Child—Choir 2, last four lines the same (chorus of all).

 SS1869

LET YOUR PRAISES RING

by Helen Kitchell Evans

Choir 1: Christ, the Lord, is risen!

Chorus: Let your praises ring!

Choir 2: Tell the wondrous story,

Chorus: Let your praises ring!

Choir 1: Sing with hearts and voices,

Chorus: Let your praises ring!

Choir 2: Christ is risen in glory,

Chorus: Let your praises ring!

Choir 1: Shout loud the glad refrain,

Chorus: Let your praises ring!

Choir 2: Christ is risen again!

Chorus: Let your praises ring!

EASTER MORNING

by Helen Kitchell Evans

Choir 1: Beautiful Easter morning!
Choir 2: Beautiful Easter Day!
Choir 1: The glory of God shown down
Choir 2: As the stone was rolled away.
Chorus: BEAUTIFUL, GLORIOUS EASTER DAY!
Choir 1: Jesus, our Lord, had risen
Choir 2: To go to heaven above;
Choir 1: Jesus, our Lord, had risen
Choir 2: To give all the world His love.
Chorus: BEAUTIFUL, GLORIOUS EASTER DAY!

SS1869

EASTER POEMS

POETRY FOR PLEASURE

Probably no nation provides as much literature for children as does the United States, yet many of our children are not reading up to their potential. If literature is to be an exhilarating educational experience the teachers need to be enthusiastic about the presentation. This is especially true of poetry. This form of dramatic interpretation requires that the teacher be sensitive to voice inflection, mood and rhythm.

Children enjoy poetry which is closely related to their thoughts, feelings, images and perceptions of their own world of experience. They like poems that tell stories, make them laugh, nonsense rhymes, and poems which present pictures of beauty.

By the time a child arrives at school, he/she has most likely begun to enjoy the rhythm of verses through hearing and learning the nursery rhymes. He/She often asks to have the same selection repeated time and again.

When the child arrives at school, he/she should be encouraged to write "poems," even if they are only two lines that rhyme.

No program in literature is complete without many hours of poetry. It enriches the day's living and sings its way into the minds and memories of children.

When children come to school filled with the love of rhythm, their senses attuned for the acceptance of poetry, what a shame if their inclinations are killed. Some schools fail to kindle this art form. Too often poetry becomes a dull assignment instead of joy. Poetry loses its flavor when it becomes a routine task.

The difference between poetry and recitation is quite obvious. Poetry is for the joy of learning and recitation for the joy of an audience.

Before reading poetry in the classroom, ask yourself these questions: Does this poem have something to say to the children? Can they relate to its meaning? Will it touch the mind and spirit?

Since nursery tunes are so familiar, children are delighted to try new words to the tunes that have already become a part of their musical background. Turn to page 48 and you will have fun with these new words to old tunes.

42

EASTER

by Edna Louise

Easter is time for new birth,
    For Christ becomes alive on earth.
Feel the strength He brings to you,
    As you start your life anew.
With pain Christ suffered, for us He died.
    His love can never be denied.
So we must surely live for Him;
    With courage strong our battles we'll win.
Knowing He is always by our side,
    Each step we'll take with hope and pride.
For our lessons come on Easter Day
    As a ray of hope when we turn and pray.
Never fear again; Christ set us free
    The day he died on Calvary.
And free we shall forever be
    When His hand guides our destiny.
Only Christ's teachings need we know;
    Whole we will become, fulfilled we will grow.

ETERNAL

by Edith E. Cutting

Life is eternal,
Each Easter affirms.
Birth and rebirth
Are part of its terms.

Christ's Resurrection
Gives life to all men.
In spite of each death,
We shall all live again.

KNOW

by Edith E. Cutting

Kneel, my sweet,
And say your prayers.
For whatever you ask—
Know that God cares.

GIVE A HUG

by Helen Kitchell Evans

Give someone a hug of gladness
When Easter comes along;
Give someone a happy day,
Fill someone's heart with song.

Give someone a bit of pleasure
At Easter and all of the year;
Tell them of Jesus and His love
And how He is always near.

Shining Star Publications, Copyright © 1989, A division of Good Apple, Inc.   SS1869

THE MEANING OF EASTER

by Donna Colwell Rosser

This morning, like the others,
 followed sunrise over the hill.
Gentle rays of warmth reached out
 to us, more gently, still.
Awakened, we are quiet.
 The world seemed muted, too.
We waited for a something—
 it held back—and then, we knew.
Today, unlike the others,
 holds a special memory;
That of Jesus risen
 as God meant Him to be.
Then, we smiled, the children, too,
 though they knew not why . . . .
But we would live forever
because of this day, long gone by.

I KNEW

by Edith E. Cutting

I saw a yellow crocus;
I heard a robin sing;
I felt the misty raindrops
And knew that it was spring.

I saw light come from darkness
In spite of griefs of men;
I went to church that morning
And knew Christ lived again.

EASTER SONG

by Donna Colwell Rosser

This day,
Embroidered in sunlight, and
Painted with the spring
Is a special gift to us.
Just hear the robin sing!

It's a lovely Easter song,
And He will have us share
The happy lift of heart
It can cause us there.

Give thanks to God for sharing.
Too, thanks to Christ, His son.
The sad, sad tale is ended:
The saving one, begun.

SS1869

HE IS HAILED AS KING

by Lucille B. Golphenee

Jesus came to Bethany,
    The place where Lazarus dwelt.
They made the Lord a supper
    With his sister Martha's help.
He was the man whom Jesus loved,
    And raised up from the dead.
Many came to see Him, and
    To hear what Jesus said.
Then Mary brought some ointment,
    Which had cost her quite a lot,
And poured it on the Master's feet,
    This precious bit she'd bought.
The house was filled with fragrance
    From its perfume, rare and sweet,
As Mary took her lovely hair,
    And wiped the Master's feet.
One of the Lord's disciples, Judas,
    Who had seen the deed,
Criticized the woman, for
    His heart was filled with greed.
He said, "Why all this awful waste?
    She should have sold the stuff,
And bought some food to feed the poor,
    Who've never had enough."
He said this, not that Judas cared
    One bit about the poor;
But just because he was a thief,
    The moneybag he bore.

The Master said, "Leave her alone;
    She is the thoughtful one.
For my coming burial,
    This loving deed she's done.
The poor you always have around,
    To help them, if you choose,
But I must soon be gone away;
    Your Master, you shall lose."
The next day, many people came,
    Who'd gathered for the feast.
They wanted so to see the Lord,
    From greatest to the least;
For they had heard it spread around,
    (Such joyful news to them),
That Jesus Christ, the Lord, was coming
    To Jerusalem.
They took palm branches from the trees
    And went to meet Him there,
And cried out praises to His name,
    A Kingly tribute, rare.
The Master rode upon a colt,
    So everyone might know
He had fulfilled this prophecy,
    Foretold so long ago.
The Lord was worshipped now, but soon
    He must be crucified;
Then He would be forsaken,
    And by many be denied.

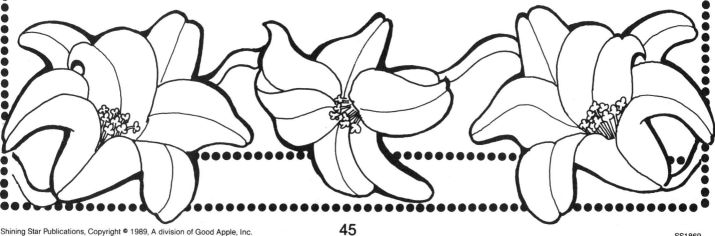

SS1869

REJOICE

by Edith E. Cutting

Lift up your hearts and be happy today;
Lift up your voices, too,
For the Father of all creation
Has given His Son for you.

Rejoice as the angels said to rejoice;
Sing till your soul shines through,
For Jesus came not just to Bethlehem,
But to every one of you.

WE LIVE

by Phyllis C. Michael

I'm going to plant a garden, you see.
  I'll watch it grow and grow.
Those tiny seeds are funny things,
  But this I'm sure you know.

I'll drop them in the warm, brown earth
  And cover them all out of sight;
I'll water them every day, then wait
  While the sun shines warm and bright.

Then soon I'll have some tiny plants,
  For deep within each seed
There's life which we can't see at all,
  But it's there, oh, yes, indeed!

And deep inside each one of you
  There's life which we can't see;
Our Saviour died and rose again
  So we'd know this could be.

Some day we'll go to live with Him.
  We'll live forevermore;
He proved this that first Easter Day,
  And FAITH is the Open Door.

SUNRISE

by Edith E. Cutting

My heart jumps up

Like a tugging kite

When I see the darkness

Give way to light.

I loose the string

And let it soar

Where the risen Christ

Has gone before.

SS1869

WHAT THE TULIPS SAY

by Phyllis C. Michael

I wonder what the tulips say
To each other as they raise their heads.
Up from the dark-brown earth they come, (1)
God calls them from their beds.

I walked quite close to them today (2)
And I thought I heard them sing,
"Praise God from whom all blessings flow; (3)
Praise God, our Lord and King."

The red one spoke (4) and the yellow ones nodded
Just as if they had done it before;
"Praise God! We live, we live, WE LIVE. (5)
We live forevermore."

(1) Tulips rise from stooping position.
(2) Speaker walks close to group and with hand cupping ear, pretends to listen.
(3) May be spoken by tulips.
(4) Red tulip says, "Praise God!" Yellow tulips nod.
(5) Spoken by all tulips as they nod in rhythm.

SS1869

MOUNTAIN FLOWERS

by Edith E. Cutting

Sung to: "The Bear Went over the Mountain"

The wildflowers bloom
On the mountain,
The wildflowers bloom
On the mountain,
The wildflowers bloom
On the mountain;
They bloom for you and me.

Yes, they bloom for you and me,
They bloom for you and me,
The wildflowers bloom
On the mountain,
The wildflowers bloom
On the mountain,
The wildflowers bloom
On the mountain;
So beautiful to see.

JOY, JOY

by Helen Kitchell Evans

Sung to: "Old Mac Donald"

Angels came on Easter Day,
Rolled the stone away;
Then Jesus walked
From out the tomb,
On that Easter Day.
There was joy, joy here,
There was joy, joy there,
Here a joy, there a joy,
Everywhere was joy, joy!
Jesus is in heaven today;
He can hear us pray.

EASTER LILIES

by Helen Kitchell Evans

Sung to: "Mary Had a Little Lamb"

Easter lilies seem to say,
Seem to say, seem to say,
Easter lilies seem to say,
CHRIST AROSE TODAY!

I PRAY

by Helen Kitchell Evans

Sung to: "Sing a Song of Sixpence"

When I pray at Easter
Dear Jesus seems so near;
It just seems that Jesus
Kneels with me here.
I am sure He hears me
When silently I pray;
For I feel a special joy
When it is Easter Day.

Shining Star Publications, Copyright © 1989, A division of Good Apple, Inc.

SS1869

EASTER PLAYS

Shining Star Publications, Copyright © 1989, A division of Good Apple, Inc.

SS1869

ON STAGE
Dramatic Interpretation

Dramatic interpretation is a way of learning through various kinds of dramatic situations. The children are helped to deepen their concepts by active, creative participation in a wide variety of experiences.

Kindergarten and primary children need challenging materials so they can learn to fully converse. Older children need materials that will enable them to have more finished productions.

Teachers who do dramatics need to be scavengers, collecting boxes, empty spools, broom handles, jewelry, purses, old clothes, etc. All of these are potential costumes and stage properties.

Situations that arise in the various areas of the curriculum are filled with opportunity for dramatization.

First—there is dramatic play, where the children dramatize a trip they have made to the post office, the firehouse or library. This type of play gives the teacher an excellent opportunity to observe the behavior of the children.

Second—there is play-making, where children develop their own lines and present their own plays.

Third—the use of puppets often helps reveal many social and emotional problems. It is often easier for a child to stand behind a puppet stage and speak through the puppet. Many children will participate in this manner when they refuse to stand before a class.

Fourth—the use of the printed plays, which is the culmination of all the other learning processes. Plays, such as those on pages 51-81, offer this type of training for the children.

To present this type of play the following instructions may be helpful:

1—Begin by reading the play to the children.

2—Be very sure that they understand the meaning of all words and have some idea of the background of the characters.

3—Read the play again, asking various children to repeat the lines (if they cannot read) or have them read various parts as you continue through the play.

4—Listen for their interpretation of certain characters before selecting the cast. If the play is being done solely for the joy of reading, a cast need not be selected. However, if being presented for the public, the best should be chosen. There will be some disappointment; but that, too, is a part of learning. All are not super in everything.

5—When parts have been selected, children must memorize before rehearsal. Do not tire the children with long rehearsal periods. It is better to have shorter periods over a longer time. We want dramatization to be a joy, not a task! Don't be afraid to try! HAPPY CASTING!

SS1869

HE KNEW!

by Edith E. Cutting

Narrator:	Samuel and Sarah have come to Jerusalem for the Passover. This evening they are sitting around the campfire eating bread and bitter herbs and roast lamb. They are with their Uncle James and Aunt Mary because they have no mother, and their father has become ill with leprosy.

Scene I

(*A campfire on the Mount of Olives.*)

Samuel:	Uncle James, do lepers have some of the Passover lamb to eat?
Uncle James:	No, I'm afraid not. Lepers are unclean.
Sarah:	(*Puts her food down.*) I don't want any more if Father can't have any.
Aunt Mary:	Now Samuel, you've spoiled your sister's supper, asking questions like that. Sarah, eat your bread, anyway. I'm sure somebody will see that your father has a good meal tonight.
Samuel:	A man I was walking beside this morning said there is a new rabbi that heals people. Do you think we could find him?
Sarah:	Yes, and ask him to heal Father.
Uncle James:	Now, children, your father isn't even here. How could this man heal him?

Sarah:	Well, I don't know how, but if he healed others—What is his name, Samuel?
Samuel:	His name is Jesus. We could ask people where he is.
Uncle James:	No, I don't want you children making a nuisance of yourselves.
Aunt Mary:	It's time we were getting to bed, anyway. Here's a blanket for each of you in case it gets cold in the night.

(Everybody lies down, Uncle James and Aunt Mary a little to the side. They are soon alseep.)

Samuel:	(*Reaching out to shake Sarah, then whispering.*) Are you awake?
Sarah:	(*Whispering*) Yes. I can't sleep. Where do you think Father is?
Samuel:	There are lights over on that hill. Do you suppose Jesus is there?
Sarah:	Oh, let's go find out. (*They throw off their blankets.*) If he is awake too, we could ask him to heal Father.
Samuel:	After Passover, when people are gone, Father could come where Jesus could touch him.
Sarah:	I don't think Jesus would have to touch him. Do you remember when we were sick? Mother just sat by us and we felt better.
Samuel:	That's right. And she wasn't even a rabbi. (*They tiptoe away.*)

SS1869

Scene II

(Jesus and two or more disciples are standing together. Samuel and Sarah enter from one side but stop as Judas, with priests and elders, enters from the other.)

Judas:	Hail, Master! (*Goes to Jesus and kisses him on both cheeks.*)
Jesus:	Friend, wherefore art thou come?
Others:	(*Shouting*) Are you Jesus? This is the one! Hold him! (*They come closer and seize Jesus. One of the disciples pulls his sword and slashes at a man.*)
Sarah:	Oh, Samuel! He cut off the man's ear! (*She covers her face with her hands.*)
Jesus:	Put up again thy sword into its place; for all they that take the sword shall perish with the sword. (*He reaches out to the wounded man.*)
Samuel:	Look, Sarah! Look! Jesus just touched his ear, and it was whole again!

(The crowd surrounding Jesus leads him away, talking and shouting. The disciples, too, run away.)

Samuel:	If we had only been here a little sooner—
Sarah:	Let's follow them. If he could heal the man's ear, he could heal our father.
Samuel:	All those men would not let us get near him. Besides, we'd better get back soon or Aunt Mary will see we're gone, and Uncle James will be angry.
Sarah:	I suppose so. (*They turn to leave.*) At least we know what Jesus looks like. We can watch for him tomorrow.

Scene III

(Morning on the Mount of Olives.)

Aunt Mary: *(Shaking one of the children and then the other.)* My goodness, you're slow this morning. Sarah! Anybody would think you didn't sleep last night. Samuel, wake up!

Samuel: We're awake now, Aunt Mary. Come on, Sarah. We watched the lights last night, so we didn't get to bed—I mean to sleep—very early.

Uncle James: Well, we'll see you get to bed earlier tonight.

Aunt Mary: Here's some bread for your breakfast, and some pressed figs. They are good to chew on.

Uncle James: We are going into the city today. There will be big crowds, so you children stay near us.

Sarah: Do you suppose we'll see the rabbi, Jesus?

Aunt Mary: No, dear. You could not get close with such crowds. You'd best forget him. We don't even know what he looks like.

Samuel: *(Smiles specially and nods at Sarah.)* Maybe he will be in the temple, and we could see him there.

Uncle James: Well, if he is, I don't want you troubling a rabbi. He will be much too busy teaching to bother with children. Now, it's time we got started.

Aunt Mary: Your uncle and I have to buy some things to take home. There's a good leather worker on a street near the temple. *(She smiles at them.)* Besides, there's a nice sweetmeat shop nearby. Maybe your uncle can spare you a penny if you're good.

Shining Star Publications, Copyright © 1989, A division of Good Apple, Inc. SS1869

Uncle James:	That's near the Antonia Fortress, and there may be trouble. One of our neighbors said there was a disturbance last night. Remember, now, stay close to us. (*They start towards the city.*)

Scene IV

(*A street in Jerusalem*)

Uncle James:	There is the temple, just ahead.
Sarah:	Maybe the rabbi, Jesus, will be teaching there.
Uncle James:	If he is, you are not to bother him. He will have weighty matters to discuss with other rabbis. Remember, now.
Samuel:	Yes, Uncle.
Aunt Mary:	You children will stay with me, anyway. Before we shop, your uncle will be going to the inner court.
	(*Sounds of crowd shouting*)
Uncle James:	Mary, listen! There must be trouble up ahead. Maybe you should take the children back.
Aunt Mary:	Not without you, James. I don't—
Samuel:	Look, look! (*Points off stage.*) The Romans are standing up in their fortress, looking over the edge.
Sarah:	Is that the governor in the middle?
Uncle James:	I do believe it is. Pontius Pilate! I wonder what can be the trouble? They are shouting so I can't hear the words.
Sarah:	Uncle James, I thought I heard the name *Jesus.*
Samuel:	And I heard *Barabbas.* Who is he?
Uncle James:	Oh, he's a troublemaker. But the governor always releases one prisoner, no matter how bad, at this feast time.
Aunt Mary:	That's probably what he's doing now. Listen!
Pontius Pilate:	(*Offstage voice*) Whom will ye that I release unto you? Barabbas or Jesus?
Sarah:	Hear that? Jesus must be there!
Samuel:	Hush!
Crowd:	(*Shouting*) Barabbas! Barabbas!
Pontius Pilate:	(*Offstage voice*) What shall I do then with Jesus?
Crowd:	(*Shouting*) Crucify him! Crucify him!
Samuel:	Crucify him? Crucify a rabbi? They wouldn't do that, would they?
Sarah:	Look at the beautiful basin his servant brought. What's that for?
Samuel:	That's strange. He's washing his hands!
Pontius Pilate:	(*Offstage voice*) I am innocent of the blood of this just man. See ye to it.
Sarah:	What does that mean?
Aunt Mary:	That he does not condemn Jesus. It's the mob of people that will be to blame.
Samuel:	You mean Pontius Pilate won't stop them?
Sarah:	Let's run closer and shout to him. He would save Father if he knew!
Uncle James:	Don't be silly. Do you think you could get through all those soldiers?
Aunt Mary:	Or even through the crowd? Hang onto my hands now.
Uncle James:	Come on into the temple. Maybe the crowd will be gone by the time we come out.

Scene V

(*The street in Jerusalem. The family is just coming out of the temple. There is the noise of a crowd in the distance, as well as people hurrying along the street.*)

Sarah:	Oh, I never saw so many people.
Samuel:	And they are all rushing so!
Aunt Mary:	Yes, I'll be glad when we get back to Galilee.
Uncle James:	Stay close to the wall and follow me. Listen! A bigger crowd must be coming. Hurry! Maybe we can get ahead of them.
Aunt Mary:	Oh, James, we're caught right in the crowd.
Sarah:	Look, Samuel. Look at that poor man! His face is all bloody. That's Jesus!
Samuel:	I think the one carrying the big cross must be Jesus.
Uncle James:	No, that's Simon of Cyrene. I know him.
Samuel:	Then the other man must be Jesus. Sarah, shall we ask—
Sarah:	(*Shakes her head.*) He's hurt. I wish I could help him! (*She stands staring at him, and suddenly Jesus raises his head and looks directly at her. For a moment there is utter silence, then the crowd moves again.*) But I'm sure he could have healed Father. (*She turns and hides her face in her aunt's robe.*)

Aunt Mary: Come now. We'll go back to the Mount of Olives. It's almost time for the Sabbath to begin. It's too late to go to the shop. We'll rest tonight, and the day after the Sabbath we'll start home.

SS1869

Scene VI

(The family is sitting around their campfire the next evening.)

Uncle James:	Well, it's been a strange time.
Aunt Mary:	Yes, we will have much to tell our friends when we get home.
Sarah:	I wish we could have talked with Jesus. I wish he hadn't died. I think he was very special.
Uncle James:	I guess you're right this time. I'm glad we were back here before it got so dark yesterday.
Aunt Mary:	And that earthquake! It's a good thing you children kept close to us.
Samuel:	Do you think it shook down any buildings in the city?
Uncle James:	Yes, I was talking with a man who got caught in the crowd. He even saw the crucifixion.
Aunt Mary:	Oh, I'm glad we didn't see that!
Uncle James:	Well, this man said the veil of the temple itself was torn.
Aunt Mary:	Really, James?
Uncle James:	Yes, and he told me something else, too. He said two criminals were crucified with this Jesus. One of them made fun of him, but the other asked Jesus to remember him when he came into his kingdom.
Sarah:	What did Jesus say?
Uncle James:	He said, "Today thou wilt be with me in Paradise!"
Sarah:	In Paradise! He could take that other man to Paradise? Then he could truly have healed Father.
Uncle James:	Well, we'll never know. He's buried now.
Samuel:	Did the Romans put him in a tomb?
Uncle James:	No, no. This man I talked with said Joseph of Arimathea—he's an important man in Jerusalem, but he lives near the place of crucifixion—this Joseph of Arimathea took down the body. Then he wrapped it and placed it in his garden in the tomb he had made for himself.
Aunt Mary:	Now, we've talked enough about such things. Tomorrow will be a new day. It's time everybody got to sleep.
Uncle James:	Yes, tomorrow we start home, and it is a long way to go.

Scene VII

(Campsite on the Mount of Olives. Everyone seems alseep. Then Sarah gets up and softly shakes Samuel. He sits up rubbing his eyes.)

Sarah:	Shhh!
Samuel:	(*Whispering*) What's the matter?
Sarah:	Let's go to the garden Uncle James told us about, where Jesus is buried. Maybe if we're just near him—
Samuel:	Uncle James and Aunt Mary won't like it.
Sarah:	Please, Samuel. We'll be back by the time they wake up, just the way we were before. (*They tiptoe out.*)

(Some time passes. It is getting lighter. Then Samuel and Sarah come running in.)

Sarah:	Aunt Mary! Aunt Mary!
Aunt Mary:	(*Sits up.*) Sarah! What's the trouble?
Uncle James:	(*Sits up.*) What's all the noise? How come you children are up?
Samuel:	Uncle James, we went to see the tomb. And it was open!
Aunt Mary:	You looked into the tomb?
Samuel:	Not till afterwards.
Sarah:	But we saw Jesus. I'm sure we did. A woman had come and she was kneeling, and she said, "Rabboni."
Samuel:	It had to be Jesus for her to call him that.
Aunt Mary:	But where was he?
Sarah:	He was standing there by the tomb. He was the man we saw by the temple, but he looks well and rested. I wanted to ask him about Father, but after he talked to the woman, he went away before I could, and she did too.
Samuel:	So then we looked into the tomb. It was empty.
Sarah:	Except for the linen clothes on one side, and a head scarf on the other.
Aunt Mary:	James, do you hear what they are saying?
Uncle James:	They must have been dreaming. Who would believe such a tale? Now it's time we got started back home.
Sarah:	No, we really did see—
Aunt Mary:	Yes, yes. Here's some bread, and we'll be on our way.
Uncle James:	The others from Galilee said they would meet us soon after sunup, and it's almost that now. Hurry!
Samuel:	But we weren't dreaming. It's true! (*They start out along the path.*)

Scene VIII

(*On the way to Galilee, about noon. The family has just finished their lunch. Aunt Mary is wrapping what is left. Sarah and Samuel walk a little way after some neighbors, then wait for their aunt and uncle.*)

Sarah:	Really, Samuel, do you think we will ever see Jesus again?
Samuel:	I don't know, Sarah. Maybe we were dreaming, as Uncle James said.
Sarah:	No, we weren't! I do wish Father were well again. He always listened when we told him things.
Samuel:	If we had only gotten to Jesus sooner—
Sarah:	But if he's alive after all, maybe he'll come to Galilee and we can ask him there.
Samuel:	Yes, and Father would be there, too.
One of the men ahead:	Look! Isn't that Samuel and Sarah's father running toward us?
Another:	It can't be. He's a leper, you know. He would not come near.
1st man:	James, isn't that your brother? The children's father?
Samuel and Sarah:	(*Running off stage.*) Father! Father! Are you well?
Father:	(*Coming onto the stage with his arms around the children.*) I am!
1st man:	Leper! Leper! (*Men back away.*)

SS1869

2nd man:	Leper! Go away! Leper!
Father:	Not any more. The priest says I am cured. One day I suddenly felt clean, so I went to the priest. There's no more sign of leprosy.
Uncle James:	Is it true? You're cured? When did it happen?
Father:	The day before the Sabbath.
Sarah:	That time Jesus looked at me! He was hurt, so I could not ask him about you, but he knew!
Samuel:	He knew! Sarah, you were right!
Father:	Who knew?
Samuel:	Jesus, the rabbi, Jesus. People said he healed ones who were sick, so we tried to ask him to heal you, but we were always too late or too far away.
Father:	Not this time! Where is this man of God that I may thank him?
Samuel:	They beat him and crucified him. It was awful. That's why we said we were too late.
Sarah:	But he's alive again. And if you said, "Thank you," I think he'd know.
Father:	Then let's all thank God indeed. Mary, James, give me your hands. I want to thank you for taking care of my children. Now we will go home, and you can tell me the whole story. But first, (*lifts his hands in prayer*) for making me well and whole again, I thank God and this beloved rabbi, Jesus! Amen!

SS1869

ANNA'S GIFT

by Marilyn Senterfitt

Setting the Scene—At stage left, place tables and chairs for the money changers. Position cardboard doves and lambs around table for animal sellers. At stage right, place a table with a box on it. The box may be spray painted gold and decorated with sequins. The temple treasury had thirteen of these chests for offerings from the people. At stage center, place two columns made of posterboard to form a doorway.

Costumes—Women wear headcoverings. Robes or housecoats can be worn by both men and women, with thongs or sandals on their feet. The widow should be dressed in tattered clothes. Anna and her mother may wear several pieces of jewelry to show their wealth.

Players—Speaking parts: Anna, Mother, Father, Jesus and three women. Nonspeaking parts: the disciples, money changers, animal sellers, various people dealing with them or giving offerings, a temple priest and the widow.

Other Props—Anna's purse, Father's large bag of coins, two pennies for the widow, numerous coins (which may be made by wrapping bottle caps in foil) and small boxes on the money changers' tables.

SS1869

THE PLAY

(*Money changers are seated at their tables. Animal sellers hold up doves and lambs. Jesus and the disciples stand, stage right, near the chest. People move back and forth between the money changers and the treasury. Some may enter stage through the doorway. Anna's father holds up a bag of coins and talks to an animal seller. Anna and her mother stand stage center.*)

Mother: The trip from Bethany to Jerusalem gets more tiresome every year. Passover season is so hectic.

Anna: Mother, can't we go to the treasury now?

Mother: No, child! We must wait for your father to purchase the lambs for our freewill offering. He is arguing the price with the sellers now.

Anna: I can hardly wait to put in my silver coin.

Mother: Anna, I thought Father gave you three coins for the treasury.

Anna: He did, but I saw that golden bracelet in the marketplace this morning. I want to get it before we go home. God will surely be just as pleased with my gift of one silver coin.

(*Anna takes the three coins out of her purse and admires them. She puts them back as her father returns.*)

Father: I got two unblemished lambs. The price was outrageous, but I was able to bring the thief down a few shekels.

Mother: There is always such an uproar at the money changers' tables.

Father: It's all the foreign travelers. They have to exchange their coins for Jewish money. As you know, only Jewish money can be put in the treasury. Those money changers try to cheat every foreigner!

Anna: Father, may we please go to the treasury now?

Father: Yes, yes. I will go into the Court of Israel after we give our gifts.

Anna: I told all my friends that you gave me three shekels to put in the chest. None of them had even given one shekel before!

(*Anna takes out one coin from her purse and approaches the chest with her parents.*)

Father: We have a generous offering to present this Passover.

(*Father holds up large bag filled with coins. People turn and watch as Anna's family gets in line. When it is his turn Anna's father makes a great show of pouring the coins into the chest. Jesus and the disciples are also watching this display. Anna holds her coin high in the air and drops it into the chest. She is very pleased with herself. She and her parents turn to leave. Anna notices that the next person in line is a poorly dressed woman. The widow moves to the chest.*)

Anna: Mother, how poor she must be. Look at her ugly clothes.

(*Mother pulls Anna away from the widow with a look of disgust on her face.*)

Mother: The poor are to be avoided. They shouldn't even be allowed in the same place as decent people.

Anna: Look, Father. She is going to give such a small gift. God will probably laugh at it!

(*The widow quietly places two pennies in the chest and walks to stage right near Jesus. Mother clutches Father's arm.*)

Shining Star Publications, Copyright © 1989, A division of Good Apple, Inc.

SS1869

Mother: John, it's the man they said brought Lazarus back to life.

(*Mother points at Jesus.*)

Father: I can't even escape that man's religious rantings in God's temple!

Mother: I don't believe for one minute he brought Lazarus back to life. It was all some kind of hoax. I never liked those sisters either.

(*Anna draws closer to Jesus.*)

Jesus: I tell you this poor widow has put in more than all of them, for they all contributed out of their abundance; but she, out of her poverty, put in all the living she had.

(*Anna returns to her parents. She is embarrassed and hides her face.*)

Anna: Oh, Father. He is talking about us!

Father: How dare he talk about a faithful Jew like that. There would be no temple if not for the rich gifts we bring! I am going to make our sacrifice. Wait for me in the Court of the Women.

(*Father goes through doorway. Anna and her mother stand stage center near doorway. Two women approach. A third woman stands nearby.*)

First Woman: That Jesus better be quiet. He will end up in Herod's prison or worse.

Mother: I agree. He's nothing more than a troublemaker.

Second Woman: I hear he has many followers among the poor. He may try to lead an overthrow of our government.

(*Third woman has been listening and now speaks up.*)

Third Woman: You are all wrong. He is wonderful!

First Woman: I suppose you believe that nonsense that he is the promised Messiah?

Third Woman: Oh, yes. I followed Him from Jericho. I've seen His miracles and listened to His teaching. He is truly God's Son.

(*The other women laugh and the woman walks away toward Jesus. During these conversations Anna has taken out her two coins and has looked over at Jesus several times.*)

Anna: Mother, I need to go back to the treasury. I won't be long.

Mother: Well, hurry. Your father will return soon and we must be home before dark.

(*Anna goes straight to the chest. She waits in line. When it is her turn she quietly places the two coins in the chest. As she turns to leave, she realizes that Jesus has been watching her. He says nothing but only smiles. Anna stands at stage center and also smiles.*)

Anna: I'm so glad that I pleased HIM!

(*Anna rejoins her mother just as her father enters through the doorway. As Anna and her parents exit stage left she turns and shyly waves to Jesus. He watches as she leaves the stage. The two women also exit stage left. The remaining people gather around Jesus. When he moves to leave they all follow and exit stage right. The money changers and animal sellers gather up their boxes and animals and exit stage left. A temple priest enters through the doorway. He picks up the chest and exits back through the doorway.*)

SS1869

HELAH, THE SCRUBBING MAID

by Edith E. Cutting

Cast of Characters:

Helah
Two guards
Jesus
Peter, a disciple of Jesus
Two messengers
Reumah, an older maid-
     servant
One person who can imitate a cock
     crowing
Other guards and servants, if desired

Setting:

The stage is divided into two parts, a courtyard and the exterior of a house.

Action:

The first scene of the play is done in pantomime. The characters pantomime as the narrator reads what is happening.

Scene I

Narrator: The last days before the Crucifixion of Jesus were very hard for His friends and disciples. During those days their faith was tested, and many turned away from Him, even Peter who had declared, ". . . I will not deny thee." Jesus had known how hard it would be for His followers, for He had warned Peter, ". . . before the cock crow, thou shalt deny me thrice."

   This play tells of Peter's denial of Jesus, as a little ten-year-old scrubbing maid in the house of the High Priest saw and heard it. She did not know of Jesus and had never seen Peter before, but she had a kind heart and a strong faith in God. It was He who sustained her when she was sold into slavery and brought here to work.

Narrator: This courtyard is that of Caiaphas, High Priest of Jerusalem. The little girl on her knees scrubbing the floor is Helah, who must clean the stones of the courtyard every night.

   While she is going on about her work, two guards march into the outdoor scene, holding between them a man with his hands tied. They clank on into the courtyard and through to the inner, official rooms of the high priest, which we cannot see.

Soon after they disappear, two messengers come running from the inner rooms, across the courtyard, and out through the garden. They are to take word to members of the high court that Jesus of Nazareth has been captured.

The two guards come back without their prisoner. They take some charcoal from a basket, and near a big cooking kettle, they start a little fire on the stones. When it begins to glow, Peter comes in. He shivers and rubs his hands as he comes hesitantly to stand by the fire, but no one pays any attention to him. After a few minutes, he sits down near the coals. Now we hear what the people have to say.

Scene II

1st Guard: I never brought in an accused man as easily as that one.

2nd Guard: I know. He didn't even try to get away. His followers ran, but he didn't even seem scared.

1st Guard: No, he had courage all right. He talked right back to that crowd.

2nd Guard: Yes, I heard him. He even asked why they hadn't taken him while he was teaching in the temple.

1st Guard: But that Judas! I hear they gave him thirty pieces of silver to point out the man they wanted.

2nd Guard: Thirty pieces of silver! Well, I hope he enjoys them! I would not give *one* piece of silver for a man that would betray his own friend—and with a kiss of greeting at that!

Reumah: (*Enters and walks towards the fire.*) Helah! Come take this kettle out and clean it. Why didn't you do that right after supper?

Helah: I'm sorry, Ma'am. I thought . . ."

Reumah: You thought! You didn't think, you mean. Hurry, now! (*She shakes her head and turns to the guards.*) You just can't get decent slaves lately, especially those from Galilee. They don't even know how to clean properly the way we do here in Jerusalem. (*Helah pulls the big kettle out of the room.*)

Reumah: (*To Peter.*) And who are you? Why aren't you working?

Peter: I don't work here. I just stopped in to warm myself by your fire.

Reumah: Oh, you're from Galilee too! I can tell by the way you talk. I suppose you were with that Jesus of Nazareth!

Peter: (*Jumps up.*) Jesus of Nazareth! I don't know what you are talking about!
(*Offstage a cock crows.*)
(*Reumah shrugs and walks across the courtyard. She sees dusty footprints on the stones where the guards came in.*)

Reumah: Helah! Come clean this floor! (*Helah enters*) Lazy thing! Why can't you do your work without somebody watching you every minute? (*Helah brings her bucket and brush and kneels to clean the floor.*) Your parents certainly didn't train you very well.

Helah: My mother and father did teach me, but they died of a sickness. My uncle sold . . ."

Reumah: Don't talk back to me! (*She yanks a lock of Helah's hair.*) I don't want to hear your troubles! Now get that floor clean. (*She comes back to the guards and points at Peter.*) This man is one of them, I tell you truly.

Peter: Them! I haven't been with anyone tonight. I just stopped here by myself to get warm. I don't know who you mean.

1st Guard: I'll tell you who she means. You're one of the followers of that Jesus we just brought in.

2nd Guard: He's from Nazareth, up in Galilee. Anyone who listens to you talk can tell you are from Galilee too.

1st Guard: What are you doing here in Jerusalem if you were not with him? I suppose you were one of those who ran away.

Peter: I swear to you, I know nothing of this man you are talking about.
(*Offstage, the cock crows again. Peter gasps. He turns and runs outside, where he stumbles and falls. Reumah and the guards chase after him to the doorway, laughing as he falls. Then they come back. Reumah goes into the inner rooms, and the guards sit or lie down by the fire to sleep.*)

Shining Star Publications, Copyright © 1989, A division of Good Apple, Inc. SS1869

Scene III

Narrator: Helah stops scrubbing as she remembers how unhappy she had been and how people had laughed at her when she was first brought to Jerusalem. She puts down her scrubbing brush, gets up and tiptoes over where she can look outside. There she can see Peter lying flat on the ground, and she hears him sobbing, the way her little brother used to do when he had hurt himself. Even though Peter is a big man and she is just a little girl, she goes out and kneels down beside him.

Helah: Are you wounded, sir? Did the guards hurt you?

Peter: Not the guards, the cockcrow.

Helah: The cockcrow could not hurt you!

Peter: No, but it made me remember something. Jesus warned me, but I forgot. (*He sits up.*) He said before the cock crowed twice I would deny Him thrice. And now I have done so. I have denied the Christ, the Messiah! How could I do such a thing?

Helah: You mean the Messiah has come? The one my father and mother looked for?

Peter: Yes, child, yes, and all the others of our nation. Jesus of Nazareth is the Messiah.

Helah: Jesus of Nazareth! But that is the man the guards brought in. He passed by me. If I had known, I could have touched His robe.

Peter: You did not know. But I knew. I was sure. (*He stands up.*) I had faith, but tonight I was afraid.

Helah: Jesus of Nazareth! You're sure he is the Messiah? Why did the guards seize him? You're sure he is not a criminal?

Peter: Of course he is not. Could you not tell by His face? So strong and gentle. But why should I blame you, little one, for not knowing, when I knew—I *knew*—and still I said I didn't.

Helah: Then we have seen Him! You and I have seen the Messiah! Oh, what shall we do? Should we tell the high priest?

Peter: It is too late. They would not let me in now. I should have gone with Him. I should have . . . .

Helah: But the guards might have beaten you!

Peter: As they may beat Him! That would not have hurt like my denial. The stripes would have healed. I am ashamed. I have hurt Him and hurt myself. No one can heal those wounds.

Helah: Can I not help?

Peter: You have already helped me, child, You have let me declare to someone that Jesus of Nazareth is in truth the Messiah. (*He puts his hands on her head.*) May the Lord bless thee and keep thee.

Helah: (*She looks up at him and smiles.*) That's the benediction we always used to say at home. Let's say it all, together.

Peter: No, I do not deserve such a benediction, for I have been unfaithful to my Lord.

Helah: (*Stands.*) My father taught me that we don't ask a blessing because we deserve it but because we need it.

Peter: And he was right. Let us indeed say it together, for I am in sore need.

Helah and (*Joining hands.*)
Peter: The Lord bless thee and keep thee:
The Lord make His face to shine upon thee, and be gracious unto thee:
The Lord lift up His countenance upon thee, and give thee peace.

SS1869

THE UPPER ROOM

by Marilyn Senterfitt

(*Narrator stands at stage left. Unrolls scroll and begins.*)

Narrator: Joel's parents were innkeepers. Their small inn was located in Jerusalem. Joel helped his parents in many ways. He arose early each morning to begin his chores. Even now he can hear his father calling across the courtyard.

(*Joel enters from left stretching and yawning. Father enters from right.*)

Father: Joel! Joel! I need you. Come immediately.

Narrator: Joel knew his father wanted him to bring water from the well. His mother was in the midst of preparing the morning meal for their guests. Joel hurried, but he never hurried fast enough for his father.

(*Joel hurries across stage to Father.*)

Father: Joel, you are as slow as a snail! I need the water pitchers filled, now!

Joel: Yes, Father. (*Father exits right. Joel picks up two pitchers from table and goes to well. He pretends to draw up water and pours it into pitchers.*)

Narrator: Joel understood that his father was always irritable during Passover season. This was a busy time for him with so many to serve and look after. The sun was just beginning to peek over the courtyard wall as Joel drew the last pitcher of water. It was Sunday, and Joel enjoyed the early hours of the day most of all. The streets were quiet, and many people still slept.

Joel: The air smells so good this morning! I wish it could be this time of day all day long! (*Joel carries pitchers toward table.*)

Narrator: As he crossed the courtyard, Joel gazed up at the window of the upper room of the inn. On Thursday evening he had helped to prepare and serve the Passover meal for the men and their leader. So much had happened since then.

Shining Star Publications, Copyright © 1989, A division of Good Apple, Inc.

SS1869

(*Joel's mother enters right and sits at table kneading dough in large bowl.*)

Joel: Mother, are the men coming down for their morning meal?

Mother: I don't think so, Joel. They are all acting like frightened children. They are afraid they will be arrested like He was and be crucified.

Joel: Do you think their Master was really the Messiah?

(*Mother kneads the dough with more vigor.*)

Mother: Of course not! Would the Messiah let His enemies treat Him the way they did that man? The Messiah would have destroyed them all, and I would not be here kneading bread at the crack of dawn!

(*Mother exits right, carrying bowl. Joel begins sweeping the courtyard. He looks left once more to upper room.*)

Joel: I wish I could have heard everything He said that night as they ate together and broke the bread. He had such a gentle way. They shouldn't have killed Him!

(*Mary enters from right.*)

Narrator: Suddenly a woman came rushing into the courtyard. Joel recognized her as one of the women who followed Him. Without a word, she rushed past Joel and went to the upper room. She knocked loudly and the door opened very slowly.

John: Mary! What has happened? You're as white as a sheet. (*John takes Mary's hand and leads her into room offstage.*)

Narrator: The door closed and Joel could hear no more. He continued with his sweeping. In a few moments, the door once again opened and two men came flying into the courtyard. Joel knew that the one man was the fisherman. He had told him about fishing in the Sea of Galilee. Joel liked him very much. The other man was also a follower.

(*Joel follows them to stage right and watches John and Peter leave.*)

Joel: They must not be afraid now. They're running right down the middle of the street!

(*Mary enters left and runs past Joel, following John and Peter.*)

Joel: I wonder why they are all in such a hurry. Oh well, I'd better wash the morning dishes. (*Joel exits right and returns with bowl and dishes. He sits at table and begins washing.*)

Narrator: The morning stretched on and Joel's parents found more and more for him to do. He had almost finished the dishes when the two men returned and went straight to the upper room. They had a strange look on their faces. Joel went inside to put up the dishes. When he returned to the courtyard, he saw the woman sitting alone by the well. Joel approached her.

Joel: May I get you some water from the well?

Narrator: At first she did not seem to hear him, and then she turned and smiled at Joel.

Mary: Yes, I would like a cup of water very much. I am thirsty.

(*Joel pretends to draw water and fills cup, handing it to Mary.*)

Joel: I saw you when you came early this morning. You seemed so excited.

Mary: Oh, I didn't even see you. I was so anxious to tell the disciples that the Master's body was gone from the tomb.

Joel: You mean someone has stolen it?

Mary: I thought that at first. Peter and John ran to the garden, and they looked inside the tomb and saw for themselves that the body was gone.

Joel: It is an awful thing that has happened.

Mary: But you don't know what has happened.

Joel: What is it?

Mary: I saw Him!

Joel: Saw whom?

Mary: I saw my Master alive. He is risen just as He said He would!

Joel: That can't be! People can't come back to life.

Mary: The Son of God can!

Joel: How can you be so sure it was really Him that you saw?

Mary: He spoke to me, called me by name. He told me to come here to the disciples and tell them the wonderful news. I must go now and do just that! (*Mary jumps up and hurries to exit left.*)

Narrator: Joel wished that he could hear more of what she had to say, but his mother was calling him.

(*Mother enters right.*)

Shining Star Publications, Copyright © 1989, A division of Good Apple, Inc.

SS1869

Mother: Joel, please come and help me serve the noon meal.

Narrator: Joel crossed the courtyard and reluctantly went inside. Later in the afternoon, Joel had an opportunity to once more speak to the woman. (*Joel enters right and Mary, left. They meet again at the well.*)

Joel: Would you tell me more about your Master?

Mary: Why don't you come to our room after supper and then you can hear in person what we have heard and seen as we followed Him.

Joel: That would be wonderful! I'll come as soon as I finish my work.

(*Joel exits right. Mother and Father enter right and move table and chair to join chair in center. Mother and Father exit right carrying cup, broom, and any other props. Peter, John, and other disciples, men, and women enter from either left or right. They gather in small groups. Mary sits at table. Joel enters right and also sits down.*)

Narrator: Later that evening Joel entered the room. There were several women gathered in quiet groups. They spoke lovingly of the Master, but tears came to their eyes when they shared their grief at His death.

(*Many begin to cry and hang their heads in sorrow. Mary stands.*)

Mary: You must believe. He is alive! (*Joel takes Mary's hand.*)

Joel: I believe you, I only wish I could see Him again just to hear His voice once more.

Narrator: In that same moment, a wondrous thing happened. Joel felt he must be dreaming, for there in the midst of the upper room stood Jesus Christ, risen from the dead!

(*Everyone falls to their knees and looks stage left.*)

Narrator: There was a gasp from all in the room, but then He spoke to them. No one any longer doubted. The Son of God was truly risen, just as He said He would. He stayed only a little while and said He would return. The upper room was silent as each one prayed to God thanking Him for this great miracle. Joel slipped away to his own room.

(*Joel moves toward right. He is smiling broadly.*)

Joel: Never in my whole life will I forget this day!

(*Joel exits and everyone else continues to pray.*)

Narrator: It is written: Jesus did many other miraculous signs in the presence of His disciples, which are not recorded in this book. But these are written that you may believe that Jesus is the Christ, the Son of God, and that by believing you may have life in His name.

(*Everyone quietly exits stage to either left or right. Narrator rolls up scroll and exits left.*)

THE END

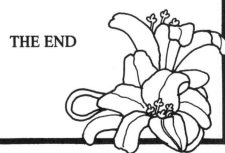

SS1869

LET'S DO A MUSICAL!

The two musical presentations that follow, PRAISE THE LORD (for primary grades) and HE IS RISEN (for upper grades), have accompanying musical scores. However, you can turn any of the plays found on pages 51-66 into musical presentations by combining them with the songs found on pages 86-90. The songs may also be used with the choral readings, poems or stories found in the first chapters of this book. Combining the original Easter songs with dramatic presentations will be fun for all those involved.

Begin rehearsing either of these musicals by having students sing all of the songs for the presentation. Practice singing only for initial rehearsals. The entire cast should learn all the verses to all the songs that will be performed. Assign solo parts where you feel your cast members have the ability and where it is appropriate. If accompaniment is not available at rehearsals, practice with taped music.

When all of the songs have been learned, begin practicing the speaking parts of the performance. Arrange to rehearse with the person that will be playing accompaniment at least two times (dress rehearsals) before the actual performance. Don't count on things going smoothly during the performance. The more practice the children have with music, scenery, and costumes the better the final performance will be.

PRAISE THE LORD
A MINI CANTATA

by Beulahmae Marchbanks

Players:

Reader 1	Robins	Sparrows	Doves
Reader 2	Bluebirds	Owls	Canaries

Music: Pianist plays "Who Shall Praise the Lord?" while everyone is being seated. (See page 72.)

Narrator: Today we invite you to share in a new experience. We invite you to attend a very special Easter sunrise service in the garden of Gethsemane. Everyone is welcome.

Reader 1: It is just breaking day in the garden of Gethsemane. The sky is turning pink from the sunrise. All the birds are awakening. They look forward to singing for the host of visitors and pilgrims who come to the garden during the day and often do not leave until late evening.

But this day is different from the others. The birds are up earlier than usual so they can have a special sunrise service of their own before any people arrive at the garden. The Lord Jesus Christ's birth, His life, His death, and His Resurrection all have special meaning for each of the birds. Let us listen . . . and remember . . . and rejoice with them.

Song: All sing "Who Shall Praise the Lord?" (See page 72.)

Reader 2: "Praise ye the Lord. Praise ye the Lord from the heavens: praise him in the heights. Praise ye him, all his angels: praise ye him, all his hosts. Praise ye him, sun and moon: praise him, all ye stars of light. Praise him, ye heavens of heavens, and ye waters that be above the heavens. Let them praise the name of the Lord: for he commanded, and they were created. Praise the Lord from the earth . . . flying fowl:" (Psalm 148:1-5, 7, 10)

Robins: Sing "Harbingers of Spring." (See page 73.)

Reader 1: "Behold the fowls of the air; for they sow not, neither do they reap, nor gather into barns; yet your heavenly Father feedeth them. Are ye not much better than they?" (Matthew 6:26)

Bluebirds: Sing "I'm Glad I Am a Bluebird." (See page 74.)

Reader 2: "Make a joyful noise unto God, all ye lands: Sing forth the honour of his name: make his praise glorious." (Psalm 66:1)

Sparrows: Sing "Only a Sparrow." (See page 75.)

Reader 1: "Are not two sparrows sold for a farthing? and one of them shall not fall on the ground without your Father. But the very hairs of your head are all numbered. Fear ye not therefore, ye are of more value than many sparrows." (Matthew 10:29-31)

Owls: Sing "Solomon, the Wise Old Owl." (See page 76.)

Reader 2: "Jesus therefore, knowing all things that should come upon him, went forth, and said unto them, Whom seek ye? They answered him, Jesus of Nazareth. Jesus saith unto them, I am he. And Judas also, which betrayed him, stood with them." (John 18:4,5)

SS1869

Doves: Sing "Just a White Dove." (See page 77.)

Reader 1: "Now when all the people were baptized, it came to pass, that Jesus also being baptized, and praying, the heaven was opened, And the Holy Ghost descended in a bodily shape like a dove upon him, and a voice came from heaven, which said, Thou art my beloved Son; in thee I am well pleased." (Luke 3:21, 22)

Reader 2: "For John truly baptized with water; but ye shall be baptized with the Holy Ghost not many days hence. But ye shall receive power, after that the Holy Ghost is come upon you: and ye shall be witnesses unto me both in Jerusalem, and in all Judaea, and in Samaria, and unto the uttermost part of the earth. And when he had spoken these things, while they beheld, he was taken up; and a cloud received him out of their sight." (Acts 1:5, 8, 9)

Canaries: Sing "Sing, Sing, Sing." (See page 78.)

Reader 1: "Let not your heart be troubled: ye believe in God, believe also in me. In my Father's house are many mansions: if it were not so, I would have told you. I go to prepare a place for you. And if I go and prepare a place for you, I will come again, and receive you unto myself; that where I am, there ye may be also." (John 14:1-3)

Reader 2: "For the Lord himself shall descend from heaven with a shout, with the voice of the archangel, and with the trump of God: and the dead in Christ shall rise first: Then we which are alive and remain shall be caught up together with them in the clouds, to meet the Lord in the air: and so shall we ever be with the Lord. Wherefore comfort one another with these words." (I Thessalonians 4:16-18)

Finale: All sing "Who Shall Praise the Lord?" (See page 72.)

 SS1869

WHO SHALL PRAISE THE LORD?

Words and Music by Beulahmae Marchbanks

SS1869

HARBINGERS OF SPRING

Words and Music by Beulahmae Marchbanks

SS1869

I'M GLAD I AM A BLUEBIRD

Words and Music by Beulahmae Marchbanks

74

SS1869

ONLY A SPARROW

Words and Music by Beulahmae Marchbanks

1. I'M ON-LY A SPAR-ROW, NOT GIFT-ED OR PRET-TY BUT
2. SO OF-TEN I WISH I COULD SING LIKE A MEAD-OW-LARK OR

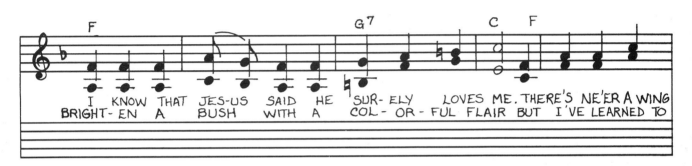

I KNOW THAT JES-US SAID HE SUR-ELY LOVES ME. THERE'S NE'ER A WING
BRIGHT-EN A BUSH WITH A COL-OR-FUL FLAIR BUT I'VE LEARNED TO

BRO-KEN OR FEATH-ER THAT FLOATS TO EARTH THAT MY HEAV'N-LY
BE CON-TENT JUST PRAIS-ING HIM EV-RY DAY IN MY OWN WAY

FATH-ER CAN-NOT FEEL OR SEE.
WHERE I AM FOR JES-US IS THERE.

NOTE: LEFT-HAND ACCOMPANIMENT— PLAY CHORD OR OCTAVES AT BEGINNING OF EACH MEASURE OR AS INDICATED, AND HOLD. BRING OUT HARMONY IN THE TREBLE CLEF.

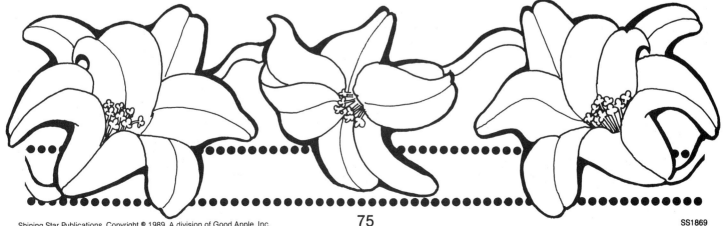

SS1869

SOLOMON, THE WISE OLD OWL

Words and Music by Beulahmae Marchbanks

Solo: 1 OWL

I AM SOL-O-MON, THE WIS-EST OLD OWL WHO LIVES HERE IN GETH-SEM-AN-E. ALL NIGHT I WATCH TO SEE WHAT HAP-PENS HERE FROM A LIMB OF AN O-LIVE TREE. I US'-LLY SLEEP ALL THE DAYS A-WAY EX-CEPT FOR THIS SPECIAL ONE. ALL THE OTH-ER BIRDS COME ONCE MORE TO SING PRAISE TO CHRIST, GOD'S RIS-EN SON.

JE-SUS USED TO COME HERE MAN-Y YEARS PAST AND IN THE GAR-DEN KNEEL AND PRAY. ALL NIGHT HE'D PLEAD FOR THIS OLD SIN-FUL WORLD, BUT THE PEO-PLE TURNED A-WAY. THEN ONE DARK NIGHT SOL-DIERS CAME FOR HIM AND THEY NAILED HIM TO A TREE. ON THE THIRD DAY HE ROSE FROM THAT COLD GRAVE. NOW HE LIVES E-TER-NAL-LY.

SS1869

JUST A WHITE DOVE

Words and Music by Beulahmae Marchbanks

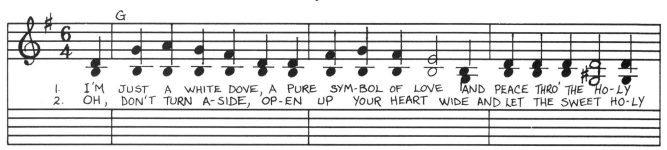

1. I'M JUST A WHITE DOVE, A PURE SYM-BOL OF LOVE AND PEACE THRO' THE HO-LY
2. OH, DON'T TURN A-SIDE, OP-EN UP YOUR HEART WIDE AND LET THE SWEET HO-LY

SPIR-IT TO-DAY. A GIFT OF GOD'S GRACE HEAV'N SENT TO RE-PLACE THE SAV-IOUR
SPIR-IT COME IN. HIS PEACE THRO' AND THRO' WILL KEEP YOUR JOY NEW AND GUARD YOU

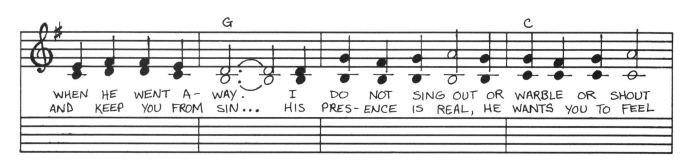

WHEN HE WENT A-WAY. I DO NOT SING OUT OR WARBLE OR SHOUT
AND KEEP YOU FROM SIN... HIS PRES-ENCE IS REAL, HE WANTS YOU TO FEEL

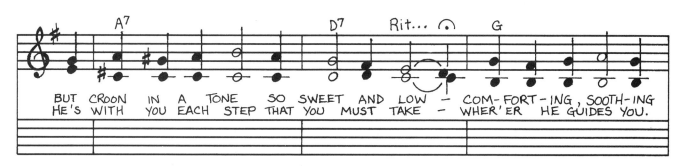

BUT CROON IN A TONE SO SWEET AND LOW — COM-FORT-ING, SOOTH-ING
HE'S WITH YOU EACH STEP THAT YOU MUST TAKE — WHER'ER HE GUIDES YOU.

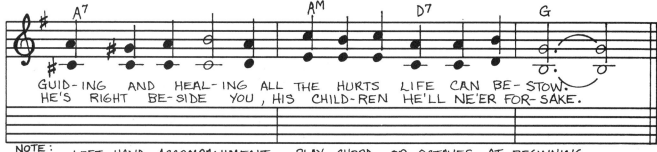

GUID-ING AND HEAL-ING ALL THE HURTS LIFE CAN BE-STOW.
HE'S RIGHT BE-SIDE YOU, HIS CHILD-REN HE'LL NE'ER FOR-SAKE.

NOTE: LEFT-HAND ACCOMPANIMENT - PLAY CHORD OR OCTAVES AT BEGINNING OF EACH MEASURE OR WHERE INDICATED. HOLD. BRING OUT HARMONY IN THE TREBLE CLEF.

SS1869

SING, SING, SING

Words and Music by Beulahmae Marchbanks

SS1869

JESUS IS RISEN!
AN EASTER OPERETTA

Play by Marilyn Senterfitt
Music by Helen Friesen

Scenery and Props: A large, freestanding room divider will be used as a backdrop. Cover both sides with newsprint or poster board. **Act I and Act III**: Draw windows showing the night sky. **Act II**: Draw a rising sun and the tomb with opening. Over opening, tape a poster board stone. **Acts I and III**: Include cups, plates, pita or French bread, fish, long table, cloth, benches or chairs. **Act II**: Props are potted palms or other greenery, small baskets.

Players: A chorus, narrator, Jesus, Twelve Disciples, three women, two servants and an angel.

Costumes: Long, tunic-like robes, headcoverings for women, white robes for Jesus and angel. Costumes may be very simple or made elaborate with colorful trims.

Act I

Setting the Scene: Place room divider with window scene facing audience. Put potted greenery behind divider. Position long table in front of the "window" and cover with cloth. Put benches or chairs along table. Chorus enters and stands stage left. At the same time, the narrator enters and stands stage right. Jesus and the Twelve Disciples enter stage right and seat themselves behind the table. Narrator begins as the two servants enter stage left and place plates, cups and bread on the table.

Narrator: It was the time of the Passover meal. Jesus gathered with His disciples in an upper room. There they remembered the night when God's angel passed over the houses of Egypt and the Hebrew people were finally freed from slavery. The traditional meal of lamb, unleavened bread and bitter herbs was served. Jesus knew that this would be His last meal with the disciples.

Jesus: (*Looks around at the disciples.*) I tell you the truth, one of you will betray me.

Disciples: (*All ask, in turn, except Judas.*) Surely not I, Lord.

Jesus: The one who has dipped his hand into the bowl with me will betray me. (*Hands Judas a piece of bread.*)

Judas: Surely not I, Rabbi?

Jesus: (*Leans toward Judas as if whispering to him.*) Yes, it is you. Go and do what you must. (*Judas hides face and exits left.*)

Chorus: (*Sing verses 1 and 2 of "Betrayed and Denied."*) (See page 82.)

Jesus: (*Holds up bread.*) Take and eat; this is my body. (*Disciples eat.*)

Jesus: (*Holds up cup.*) Drink from it, all of you. This is my blood of the covenant, which is poured out for many for the forgiveness of sins. I tell you, I will not drink from this fruit of the vine from now on until that day when I drink it anew with you in my Father's kingdom. (*Disciples drink.*)

Chorus or Jesus: (*Sing both verses of "Communion Hymn."*) (See page 82.)

SS1869

Jesus: I shall not be with you much longer. I give you a new commandment: Love one another; just as I have loved you, you also must love one another. By this love you have for one another, everyone will know that you are my disciples.

Chorus or Jesus: (*Sing "Love One Another."*)

Peter: (*Moves closer to Jesus.*) Lord, where are you going?

Jesus: Where I am going you cannot follow me now.

Peter: Why can't I follow you? I will lay down my life for you.

Jesus: Lay down your life for me? I tell you most solemnly, before the cock crows you will have disowned me three times. (*Peter, with head down, returns to his seat.*)

Chorus: (*Sing verses 2 and 4 of "Betrayed and Denied."*)

Narrator: When the Passover meal was completed, Jesus and the disciples sang a hymn and went out to the Mount of Olives. Jesus knew He would soon be arrested and the next day would be nailed to the cruel cross.

Jesus and Disciples: (*Sing "Love One Another." Leave the table and exit right.*)

Chorus: (*Continue to sing "Love One Another" as two servants enter stage left and clear table. Conclude when servants exit left.*)

Act II

Setting the scene: The tomb in the garden. Chorus members move table and benches to stage right. They turn the divider around and place greenery on either side. The angel stands behind divider.

Narrator: It was early on Sunday morning. Mary, the mother of James, Joanna and Mary Magdalene came to the garden bringing sweet spices to place in the tomb. (*Women carry small baskets and enter stage left.*)

Mary: How will we be able to roll the stone away from the door of the tomb?

Joanna: I don't know. The stone is very heavy. (*Simulate earthquake. The women sway back and forth. They drop their baskets and fall to ground. If possible, the angel moves divider. Angel then walks around to front of divider, removes cardboard stone and steps to the side.*)

Mary Magdalene: (*Rises to her feet.*) Look! The stone is rolled away! (*They run to the tomb and look inside. They step back in fear as they see the angel.*)

Angel: Do not be afraid. You are looking for Jesus of Nazareth, who was crucified. He is not here. He is risen. Go tell the disciples. (*Joanna and Mary exit stage left. Angel exits stage right. Mary Magdalene starts off stage left and hesitates. She is met by Peter and John.*)

Mary Magdalene: They have taken the Lord from the tomb. We don't know where they put Him. (*Peter and John run to the tomb. John arrives first. Peter looks inside.*)

Peter: There are the linen cloths they wrapped Him in, but His body is gone!

John: What can this mean? Could Jesus have risen from the dead? (*Shaking their heads in wonder they exit stage left, passing Mary Magdalene. She moves to stage center. As chorus sings she moves to look once more in the tomb.*)

Chorus: (*Sing both verses of "Jesus Arose."*)

Jesus: (*Enters stage right, wearing a white robe, with red marks on hands and feet. Approaches Mary*

Magdalene.) Woman, why are you crying? Who is it you are looking for?

Mary Magdalene: (*Does not recognize Jesus.*) Sir, if you have carried Him away, tell me where you have put Him, and I will get Him. (*Turns her back to Jesus and cries even more.*)

Jesus: Mary.

Mary Magdalene: (*Turns at the sound of her name and falls to Jesus' feet.*) Teacher!

Jesus: Go to my brothers and tell them, I am returning to my Father and your Father, to my God and to your God. (*Jesus exits stage right.*)

Chorus or Mary Magdalene: (*As Jesus and Mary Magdalene exit, chorus sings all verses of "Love My Jesus"; or Mary Magdalene moves to stage center and sings all verses of "Love My Jesus" and then exits stage left.*) (See page 84.)

Act III

Setting the Scene: The upper room. Chorus members turn divider and place greenery behind it. Move benches or chairs in front of divider. Have plate with fish on table. Disciples enter stage right and either sit or stand.

Narrator: Later on that glorious Sunday the disciples once more gathered in the upper room. Thomas had not joined them. The disciples were frightened and confused. They drew back in fear at the frantic knocking on the locked door. (*Knock on wood offstage.*) Andrew cautiously opened it and the women came rushing into the room.

Chorus or Women: (*Sing verses 1 and 2 "Hosanna!"*) (*See page 84.*)

Peter: Yes, I did find the tomb empty. John and I aren't sure what has happened.

Jesus: (*Jesus enters stage left. Disciples and women are frightened, and many bow down before Him.*) Peace be with you. Why are you afraid? Why do you doubt? (*Holds out His hands.*) Look at my hands and feet and see that it is I, Myself. Touch me and you will know, for an angel doesn't have flesh and bones, and I have. (*They gather around Jesus and touch His hands, face and arms.*)

John: I see you, Lord, with my own eyes, but do you really live?

Jesus: Do you have anything here to eat?

Andrew: (*Goes to table and brings plate with fish.*) We have some fish, Lord. (*Jesus eats fish.*)

Peter: Angels do not eat. Our master lives!

Jesus: (*Hands Andrew the plate.*) Truly I tell you, I will be with you always, even unto the end of time.

Chorus and Entire Cast: (*Jesus stands stage center, with chorus and cast around Him. Sing last verse of "Hosanna!" using optional 3rd ending.*) (See page 84.)

(*With music being quietly played, chorus exits stage left and remaining cast exits stage right. Jesus stands stage center for a moment. As he exits stage right, conclude by playing joyous version of "Hosanna!" using the optional 3rd ending.*)

Shining Star Publications, Copyright © 1989, A division of Good Apple, Inc.

SS1869

BETRAYED AND DENIED

Words and Music by Helen Friesen

1. WE SAY WE LOVE HIM, WE TRY TO SERVE HIM, STILL WE AT TIMES MAY FALL,
2. NO-TICE THE GUILT THAT JU-DAS THEN CARRIED, NO MON-EY COULD E-RASE,
3. WHILE THEY WERE SIN-NING, JE-SUS STILL LOVED THEM, HOW COULD THEY HURT HIM SO?
4. PE-TER RE-PENT-ED, WEPT TEARS OF AN-GUISH, WATCHED HOW HIS MAS-TER BLED,

1. JU-DAS BE-TRAYED HIM, PE-TER DE-NIED HIM, THERE AT THE JUDGE-MENT HALL.
2. TRIED TO RE-TURN IT, BUT THEY RE-FUSED IT, HIS LIFE HE COULD NOT FACE.
3. WE MAY FOR-GET THAT JE-SUS CAN SEE US, NO MAT-TER WHERE WE GO.
4. JE-SUS FOR-GAVE HIM, GAVE HIM A MIS-SION, "GO FEED MY LAMBS," HE SAID.

COMMUNION HYMN

Words and Music by Helen Friesen

1. TAKE THIS BREAD I GIVE TO YOU, EAT IT AND RE-MEM-BER ME,
2. TAKE THIS CUP I GIVE TO YOU, DRINK IT AND RE-MEM-BER ME,

BRO-KEN LIKE MY BOD-Y TOO, EAT IT AND RE-MEM-BER ME.
LIKE MY BLOOD WAS SHED FOR YOU, DRINK IT AND RE-MEM-BER ME.

SS1869

LOVE ONE ANOTHER
Words and Music by Helen Friesen

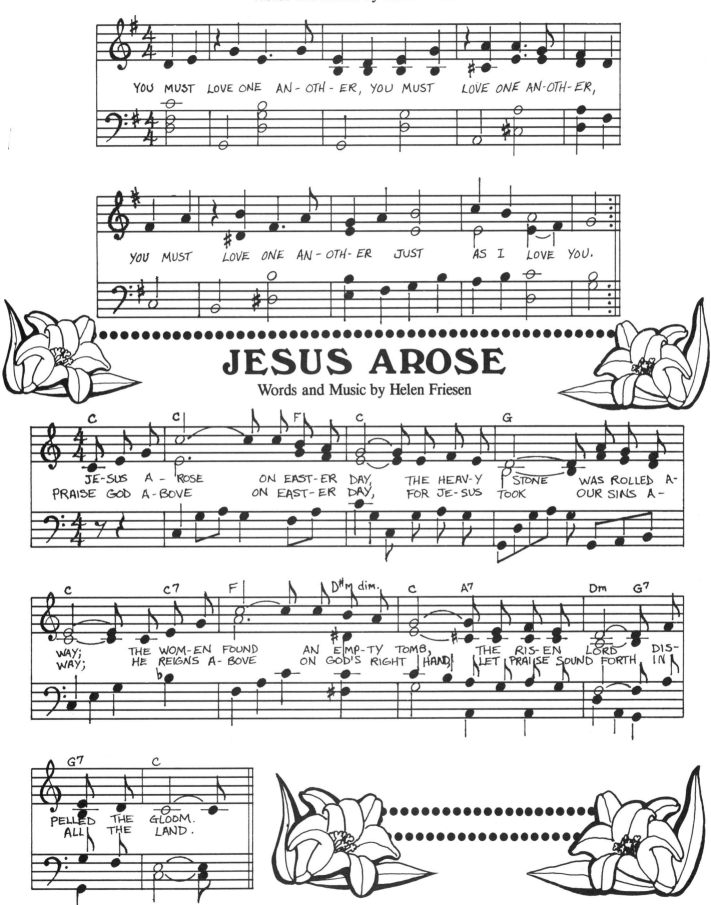

YOU MUST LOVE ONE AN-OTH-ER, YOU MUST LOVE ONE AN-OTH-ER,

YOU MUST LOVE ONE AN-OTH-ER JUST AS I LOVE YOU.

JESUS AROSE
Words and Music by Helen Friesen

JE-SUS A-ROSE ON EAST-ER DAY, THE HEAV-Y STONE WAS ROLLED A-
PRAISE GOD A-BOVE ON EAST-ER DAY, FOR JE-SUS TOOK OUR SINS A-

WAY; THE WOM-EN FOUND AN EMP-TY TOMB, THE RIS-EN LORD DIS-
WAY; HE REIGNS A-BOVE ON GOD'S RIGHT HAND, LET PRAISE SOUND FORTH IN

PELLED THE GLOOM.
ALL THE LAND.

SS1869

LOVE MY JESUS

Words and Music by Helen Friesen

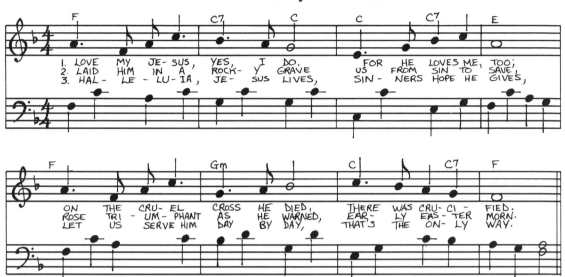

1. LOVE MY JE-SUS, YES, I DO, FOR HE LOVES ME, TOO;
2. LAID HIM IN A ROCK-Y GRAVE, US FROM SIN TO SAVE;
3. HAL-LE-LU-IA, JE-SUS LIVES, SIN-NERS HOPE HE GIVES,

ON THE CRU-EL CROSS HE DIED, THERE WAS CRU-CI-FIED.
ROSE TRI-UM-PHANT AS HE WARNED, EAR-LY EAS-TER MORN.
LET US SERVE HIM DAY BY DAY, THAT'S THE ON-LY WAY.

HOSANNA!

Words and Music by Helen Friesen

HO-SAN-NA, HO-SAN-NA, THE EARTH-QUAKE SHOOK THE GROUND THE STONE WAS ROLLED A-WAY; HO-SAN-NA,
FOR CHRIST IS RIS-EN TO-DAY,

HO-SAN-NA, NO BOD-Y THERE WAS FOUND FOR MAR-Y SAW THE
THE GRAVE-CLOTHES STILL THERE LAY WHEN HE ROSE TRI-UM-PHANT
GOD'S SON DID HIM O-BEY;

TOMB WAS BARE, "WHY IS-N'T JE-SUS' BOD-Y THERE?"
TOMB HAD FLED, HE FOUND IT JUST LIKE MAR-Y SAID, HO-SAN-NA, HO-
FROM THE GRAVE, HE LIVES FOR-EV-ER US TO SAVE,

1ST AND 2ND AND OPTIONAL 3RD ENDING. | OPTIONAL 3RD ENDING.

SAN-NA, RE-JOICE WITH US TO-DAY! | RE-JOICE WITH US TO-DAY!

SS1869

EASTER SONGS

How will you present the original songs that follow? Will they be sung as an Easter performance? Will a few of them be used to turn your Easter play into a musical? Or will they be part of a choral reading recitation? Any way you choose to use the original songs that follow, the children are sure to enjoy singing them, because each song was written especially for young children.

You may wish to begin by singing all the songs with your students. (See additional Easter songs for children, found on pages 32, 72-78 and 82-84.) Decide which songs the children enjoy singing the most. Let them decide which ones they would like to perform and how they want to include the songs in the Easter production. If musical instruments (example, bells) are to be part of the performance, have the children practice with the instruments after the first few rehearsals.

Decide where the songs will be used if using them with a play. Sing them between different scenes, and decide where they will work best with your group. Youngsters have very good ears for this sort of thing, so be sure to listen to their input. Experiment; play some of the songs softly in the background during narrations. Would that add to the quality of your performance? Can songs be played softly before and after the performance as the audience is entering and leaving the auditorium? You may want to make copies of the songs so the audience can join in and sing some songs during or after the performance.

How you use the songs will depend on your performance. Be imaginative and let the children help make some of the decisions. Anyway you choose to use the songs that follow, they will make the Easter season more joyous.

Arranged by Shirley Schirmer

BLESSED IS HE

Words by Helen Kitchell Evans
Music by Joe Anne Berkel

HO - SAN - NA! HO - SAN - NA! BLESS-ED IS HE THAT COM-ETH IN THE
NAME OF THE LORD — EN - TER IN-TO HIS GATES WITH THANKS-GIV-ING AND
IN-TO HIS COURTS WITH PRAISE BE THANK-FUL UN-TO HIM AND BLESS HIM
FOR THE LORD IS GOOD AND HIS TRUTH EN-DUR-ETH FOR EV - ER.

86

SS1869

IN OUR HEARTS

Words by Helen Kitchell Evans
Music by Joe Anne Berkel

SS1869

UP FROM THE GRAVE

Words by Helen Kitchell Evans
Music by Frances Mann Benson

SS1869

HE IS NOT HERE, HE IS RISEN

Words and Music by Vickie Garrison

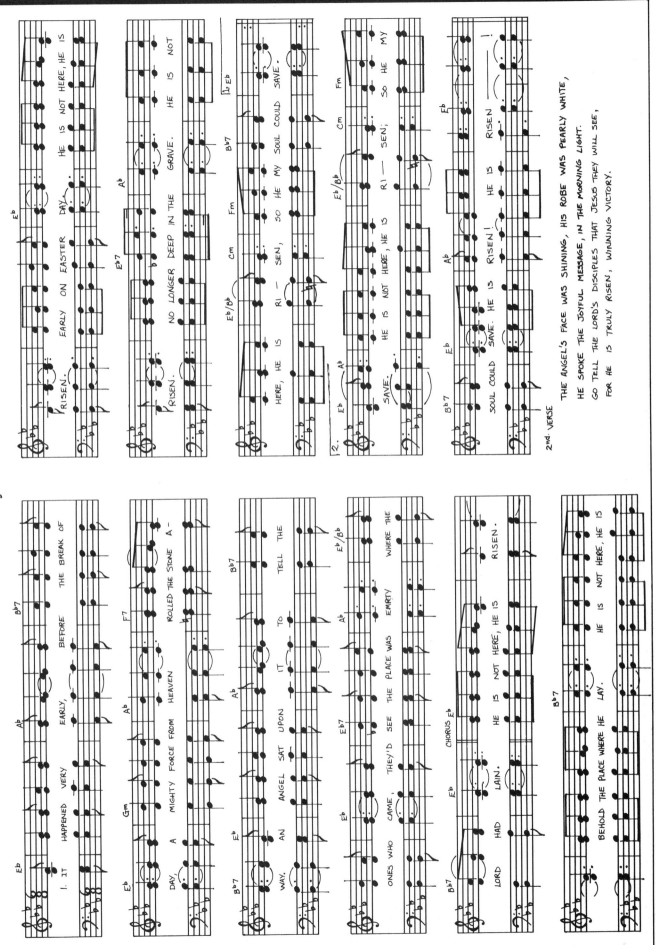

THE ANGEL'S FACE WAS SHINING, HIS ROBE WAS PEARLY WHITE,

HE SPOKE THE JOYFUL MESSAGE, IN THE MORNING LIGHT.

GO TELL THE LORD'S DISCIPLES THAT JESUS THEY WILL SEE,

FOR HE IS TRULY RISEN, WINNING VICTORY.

SS1869

THANK YOU, LORD, FOR SPRING THINGS

Words and Music by Kay Stewart
Arranged by Shirley Schirmer

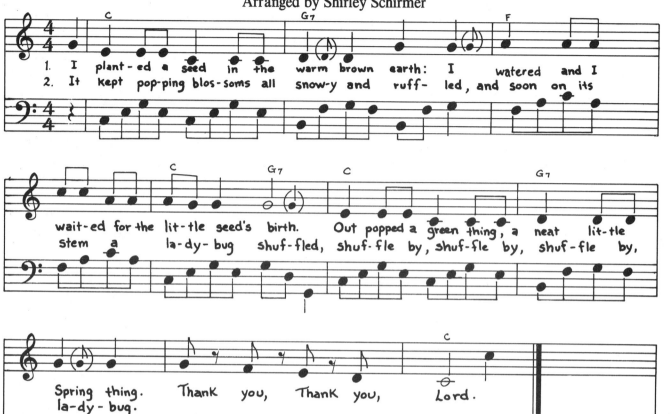

I planted a seed in the warm brown earth. (*Drop an imaginary seed with right hand into opening of fist next to thumb on vertical left hand.*)

I watered and I waited for the little seed's birth. (*Pretend to hold sprinkling can in right hand and to pour water into thumb nest.*)

Out popped a green thing, a neat little spring thing. (*On the word "popped," hold up thumb.*)

Thank you, thank you, Lord. (*Palms together, fingers steepled in prayer.*)

It kept popping blossoms (*Left hand back in vertical position as before, springing fingers up to join thumb on words "popping blossoms."*)

All snowy and ruffled, (*Wiggle fingers, palm held flat open.*)

And soon on its green stem a ladybug shuffled. (*Move left arm upward in vertical position and begin walking fingers of right hand from elbow toward left hand, straight up.*)

Shuffle by, shuffle by, shuffle by, Ladybug. (*Stop fingers in middle of left palm on the word "ladybug" after shuffling fingers all the way up arm.*)

Thank you, thank you, Lord. (*Palms together, fingers steepled in prayer.*)

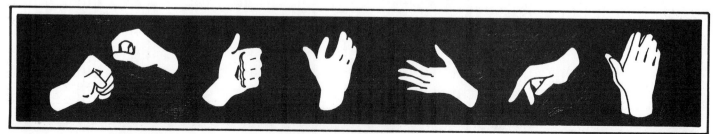

COSTUMES AND SCENERY
The Finishing Touches!

On the following pages you will find suggestions and patterns for making simple costumes and scenery for Easter performances. Remember to keep it simple. If costumes become too elaborate and the scenery and props too complicated, it will detract from the overall beauty of the Easter story. To keep costs down, use what you have on hand or ask for donations before you purchase anything. Use your imagination. The best source of ideas is right in your own head and the children's heads. Put your heads together, look around, and you'll be amazed at the great costume and scenery ideas you will develop. Getting ready for the performance should be as much fun as the big production.

Use an overhead projector to enlarge any of the patterns found on pages 94, 95 or 96 for backdrops or stand-up scenery. Trace the patterns you want to enlarge on some clear transparency material and place it on your projector. Then you are ready to make your illustrations as large or as small as you desire. You can project the images directly onto cardboard, wood or whatever material you are using.

Shining Star Publications, Copyright © 1989, A division of Good Apple, Inc.

SS1869

BASIC ROBES

A twin-size sheet can be used to make a loose-fitting costume. Use stripes and solid dark colors for the boys and solid pastel colors for the girls. Fold sheet in half lengthwise. Fold again from top to bottom. Cut a pattern like the one shown. Adjustments can be made for hem and arm length for each child. Stitch the side seam and under the arm. Raw edges may be hemmed by turning up once. For more color, braid or fringe can be added at neckline or hems. Tie at the waist with cord or man's necktie. The girls' headcoverings can be a contrasting 36″ x 36″ piece of fabric. Center on head, and hold in place with bobby pins or a stretch headband. Thongs or sandals can be worn. See sandal directions on this page.

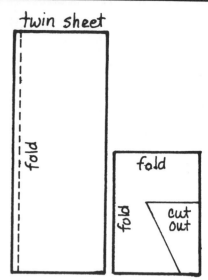

twin sheet

fold

fold

fold

cut out

20″

20″

20″

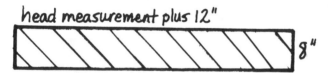

head measurement plus 12″

8″

SANDAL CRAFT

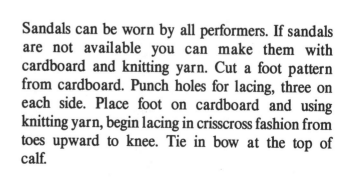

Sandals can be worn by all performers. If sandals are not available you can make them with cardboard and knitting yarn. Cut a foot pattern from cardboard. Punch holes for lacing, three on each side. Place foot on cardboard and using knitting yarn, begin lacing in crisscross fashion from toes upward to knee. Tie in bow at the top of calf.

SS1869

NARRATOR FASHIONS

The narrator should also be dressed in costume. Narration may be read from a scroll. This can be made with two dowels and a paper bag. Cut strip of paper from bag, 8″ wide and 10-12″ long. Using two 10″ dowels, glue the end of the brown paper to each. Tape narrator's part on the paper and roll up. Secure with colorful cord.

CLOTHES FOR ANGEL

Make angel costumes from white sheets, following basic robe pattern described on page 92. Gold tinsel tied around the waist and attached to the neckline will make angels glow. Gold ribbons may be tied around foreheads.

BIRD COSTUMES

Each bird costume requires a bolt of crepe paper. Cut in 1″ strips lengthwise, about three-fourths of the way to the top. Then unfold and gather the firm edge of the paper onto a 1″ piece of fabric long enough to fit around a child's neck, leaving fabric ends open 1″ from each end so it can be pinned at the back of the neck. The shreds hang like feathers over the shoulders in a cape style. Suggested colors: orange for robins, brown for owls, yellow for canaries, silver for sparrows, white for doves and blue for bluebirds.

EASTER BONNETS

Simple Easter bonnets or birds' headcoverings are made with paper plates with slightly fluted edges, artificial flowers, ribbon, and a 2″ strip off the end of a bolt of crepe paper. (The rest of each crepe paper bolt can be used for the wings of birds, if you are performing PRAISE THE LORD, a mini cantata.) Staple the 2″ strip of crepe paper around the edge of the paper plate to form a ruffle. Add artificial flowers to the top. Staple a ribbon ½″ wide on the bottom of plate, long enough to come down and tie under the chin.

SS1869

SCENERY PATTERNS

Flannel board cutouts, bulletin board patterns, clip 'n' copy Easter graphics

The reproducible Easter figures that follow can be used in dozens of creative ways to make the Easter season more joyful. Here are a few tips for using the Easter graphics:

1. Use an overhead projector to enlarge play scenery. Directions are found on page 91.

2. Reproduce on light cardboard. Cut out and attach flannel strips to the back of each figure to use for telling the stories found on pages 5-24.

3. Use an overhead projector to enlarge figures for bulletin boards.

4. Use as greeting card illustrations. Duplicate enough for each child on construction paper. Children can decorate cards with markers, crayons, paint and glitter. Use Scripture verses or phrases for greeting cards.

5. Reduce to make patterns for Easter stickers and awards. (Most print shops can reproduce copy to any size desired.)

6. Use an overhead projector to enlarge figures for a hall mural. Include all the figures in an appropriate order to tell the Easter story. Have children attach Bible verses in sequential order under pictures. Use colored chalk to make soft, pastel pictures.

7. Reproduce on light cardboard. Give each student a set of figures and yarn to create his/her own Easter mobile. Punch holes in the top and bottom of figures and tie together in a balanced fashion.

Mary

SS1869

Shroud

Sun

Angel

Mary Magdalene
and Mary

SS1869

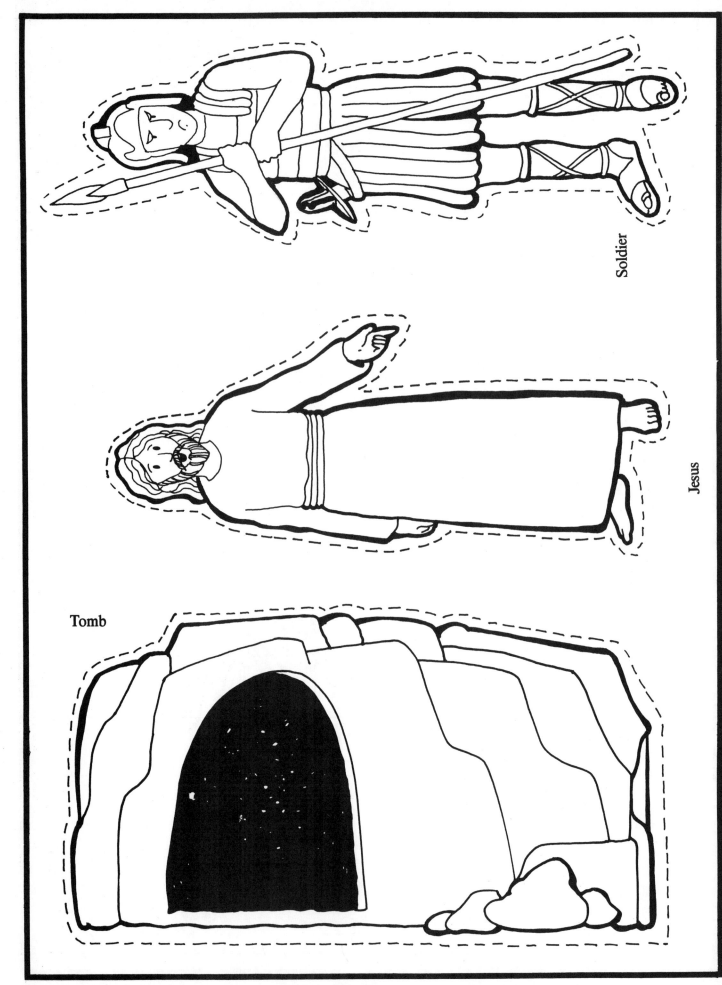

Soldier

Jesus

Tomb

96

SS1869